ZEN AND THE ART OF COACHING BASKETBALL

MEMOIR OF A NAMIBIAN ODYSSEY

BEN GUEST

PRAISE FOR ZEN AND THE ART OF COACHING BASKETBALL

I was hooked from the start. A terrific read of the can't-put-it-down variety! - Andy Clayton, Daily News

Ben takes a mediocre foreign high school team, coaches them in a way antithetical to almost every way it's been done... and the results - and the STORY (without providing the almost unbelievable ending) - are unforgettable. As good as any BASW pick! - Glenn Stout, Series Editor, The Best American Sports Writing

Zen and the Art of Coaching Basketball is a heartwarming tale of self-discovery told against the backdrop of Ben's fascinating journey through a nascent basketball culture on the other side of the world. He skillfully introduces the elements of a new paradigm for leadership on and off the court based on trust, compassion and "surrendering to what is" that contributed to a remarkable upset by an endearing young basketball team. - Paul Knepper, The Knicks of the Nineties

Coaching is about vulnerability. I appreciate the vulnerability that Ben embodied within his story. This book is a

must-read for a coach at any level, as it will help you reflect on where you got your coaching style from, how you have implemented it, and most importantly does it center players and empower them or just control them. Coaching has changed within the last decade but coaches continue to use methods they learned from their "old school" coaches. This book is an easy read that helps you better understand yourself through Ben's story. Well worth it. - Jen Fry, CEO, Jen Fry Talks

A modern day Hoosiers where reality trumps what even the most talented writer could dream up. - Andrés Alvarez, Editor-in-Chief, Box Score Geeks

This magical memoir offers many insights into basketball, coaching, values, team building, culture, etc. It is impossible to read without absorbing valuable life lessons, gently revealed. A captivating, well-told tale, both universal and specific, of an incredible basketball season and life journey. - Ray LeBov, Founder and Editor-in-Chief, Basketball Intelligence

Reading Zen and the Art of Coaching Basketball is like being transported to the blowing grasslands of Namibia. Everywhere you look you're confronted with mirage-like amalgams of past, present, and future. A cracked concrete

basketball court in a field of ancient wheat. A growing city in the birthplace of mankind. A white American coaching in post-apartheid Southern Africa. It's entertaining and revealing in equal measure. With fast-break speed and delicate compassion, Ben Guest weaves a breezy, engrossing story about staying present, even in life's most defining moments. - Greg Larson, Clubbie: A Minor League Baseball Memoir

Ben encourages coaches and leaders to reorient their focus and achieve incredible results. Through personal experiences in coaching and in life, Ben shows the importance of meditation, relational leadership, and understanding those you lead. Helping people reorient their focus from looking through people and only at results to truly understanding the value of people and relationships to achieve those results, Ben's narrative is a must read! Coaches and leaders will learn how to grow the impact of their leadership while also creating a caring, positive environment. - Josh Smith, Head Coach, Women's Soccer, Rogers State University

We often see coaches on the sidelines screaming at their players. The mantra of many coaches appears to be "yell, yell, and then yell some more." In "Zen and the Art of Coaching Basketball", Ben Guest offers a better way.

Teaching doesn't require yelling. Coaches who read this well-written memoir will learn that success doesn't require screaming. In fact, all that screaming has probably made your team's success less likely. - David Berri, Wages of Wins

I played for Coach Guest at Simmons High School in Hollandale, Mississippi. He helped me when I was struggling with my confidence and we're still in touch today. He's the kind of coach who provides positive feedback and makes you believe in yourself." - Larry Brown, Head Coach, Girls Basketball, Boyd H. Anderson High School, Lauderdale Lakes, FL

CONTENTS

Zen and the Art of Coaching Basketball: Memoir of a Namibian Odyssey

By Ben Guest

ZEN AND THE ART OF COACHING BASKETBALL
Memoir of a Namibian Odyssey

Author: Ben Guest
Editor: Glenn Stout
Cover: Ben Guest

First Edition published November 2021
Copyright © 2021 Ben Guest

NEWSLETTER

Join the hundreds of people who have signed up for my free weekly newsletter at benbo.substack.com for interviews with writers AND receive a FREE copy of my ebook *Lessons Learned Self-Publishing on Amazon, Working with a Professional Editor, Starting a Podcast, and Creating a Newsletter*.

This memoir is based on memories, journal entries, emails to friends and family, a video review of the games, and text messages. I have reconstructed various conversations to the best of my recollection. Some names have been changed.

To the Blue Devils. We are all connected.

PART I

You have a much too willful will. You think that what you do not do yourself does not happen.

—Eugen Herrigel, *Zen in the Art of Archery*

1

THE MOMENT

DEEP BREATH IN. Deep breath out.

I was watching my team, the Blue Devils Basketball Club, the team I coached, the team I had started from scratch, try to pull off the greatest upset in Khomas Basketball Association history.

The KBA is Namibia's professional basketball league. With a population shy of three million, Namibia, on Africa's southwest coast, is red desert to the south and east, yellow plain to the north, and ice-blue Atlantic Ocean beyond the west coast.

It was the first game of the first round of the playoffs, September 5, 2015, and my team, the Blue Devils, the lowest seed in the playoffs, was facing the Wolves, the best team in the league.

Sepo, our starting point guard, with his long arms and gentle face, had fouled out. Mike, our backup point guard, pencil-thin mustache and cocky smile, had also fouled out. I looked at the digital scoreboard and, as Mike walked off the court, took a timeout.

With two minutes left in the game, we were down three points.

The crowd at Gym Hall, the arena on the campus of the University of Namibia where KBA games were played, was delirious. Retired players, one wearing a red number twenty-three Bulls jersey, another in a green Celtics jersey, number five, yelled at the players while sipping whiskey from red plastic cups. Older women, comfortably dressed in black leggings or tan capri pants, sat together and laughed at the seriousness of their drunken husbands. Sitting one section over was the younger, hipper crowd, made up mostly of university students. The guys sat next to each other, sunglasses resting on their foreheads even though it was an evening game. Younger women sat in front, sometimes looking back at the guys with shy half smiles.

Silver hoop earrings sparkled in the sodium lights.

Apart from me, there was one other White person in the gym, the German girlfriend of a player on the Wolves. In contrast to the rowdy fans she was clapping softly to release the tension of the close game. The pressure weighed on both teams.

If we won, it would be the greatest upset in KBA history.

I looked over at the Wolves' bench. They were tense, animated, aggressive. Like the inspiration for their name, they played with a "kill or be killed" mentality.

My team, the Blue Devils, took the opposite approach. We were Zen warriors, sitting quietly and breathing deeply. Translated from Sanskrit, Zen means to remain calm and present in the moment.

Which philosophy would win?

The Wolves were the number one seed, made up of grown men, some of whom had played professionally overseas in Germany or in South Africa. In contrast, we were the youngest team in the KBA, a mix of high schoolers and recent high school graduates. The Wolves had swept us in the regular season, winning both games by double-digits. The contest should not have been close and now, with two minutes left in the game, we had no point guard.

Television cameras, set up on a riser on one side of the stands, took in everything, broadcasting digital images across the country.

The game would be won or lost in the next few moments.

I walked over to the team and nodded at Vincent Jackson.

"Vincent, you're in."

Vincent was the guy who loved being around the other guys, the first one to high-five a teammate or offer an encouraging word... and the last man on my bench. He was not the player I expected to have on the court during the deciding moments of a close playoff game.

Sometimes we choose the moment. And sometimes, well, sometimes the moment chooses us.

For Vincent Jackson, all of seventeen-years-old, playing in a men's professional league, playing in the final seconds of a pressure-packed playoff game, his moment was...

Now.

2

NAMIBIA

I FIRST MET the team a year and a half earlier, in February of 2014, on an outdoor court. Shouts and laughter from the nearby soccer game drifted over us. Wood smoke from distant cooking fires gave the air a funky smell.

The ten young men standing before me, skinny and athletic, were different from most of their friends. Instead of soccer, they were into basketball. Boxing, rugby, and soccer were the most popular sports in the country and received the most government funding. Basketball was third-tier.

I was thirty-nine years old, teaching high school English at an affluent private school. The ten Black teenagers before me had rarely experienced any affluence. They were public school kids, most from single-parent or no-parent homes. The average household income in Namibia was about $4,000 a year, and the guys I was meeting for the first time came from families on the losing end of that average. Almost every aspect of their lives was a struggle.

I had first come to Namibia seventeen years earlier, in 1997, as a twenty-two-year-old Peace Corps Volunteer. I was placed as a high school teacher in Engela, a small village far to the north of the capital city Windhoek. After my two years of service were up, I returned to the U.S. Now, fourteen years after I had completed my Peace Corps service, I was back in Namibia.

They stood there, typical high schoolers in their own way, although the jerseys and sneakers were more worn than you would find in the United States, the soles of their shoes smooth as paper. Two came to practice barefoot.

Always confident, Mike smiled, showing off his silver-capped tooth. His eyebrows arched, and he looked out with bright, clever eyes. On the cusp of manhood, he sported a pencil-thin mustache.

Sepo, all muscle and confidence with ears like satellite dishes, grinned with enthusiasm. Jack, with his close-cropped hair, was silent.

I stood across from them, a metal whistle around my neck. I wore dark sunglasses and 50 SPF sunscreen so thick it looked like toothpaste. The world, which had rolled out a red carpet of privilege for me, from private U.S. high school to elite, private, four-year college, offered these young men nothing but indifference.

We stood apart. Nervous.

Namibia is mostly desert, its population spread out over a land mass the size of Texas. Only the center of Windhoek, about six city blocks long and another six city blocks wide, home to a fifteen-story Hilton hotel, the tallest building in the country, looks like a modern city.

Surrounding Windhoek are various suburbs or, as they are referred to locally, "locations," areas where, until the end of apartheid in 1990, Black people had been forced to live. The locations are a mix of one-story houses with electricity and DSTV satellite dishes and tin shacks where people cook dinner over a wood fire. Each year, the shacks extend further and further out into the countryside, where, on occasion, a cheetah might be seen ranging along the tar road.

Fifty minutes' drive past the shacks and the landscape becomes a yellow grassy plain where women fetch precious water from wells, balancing large plastic buckets on their heads.

The distance between the past and the present isn't far.

3

PORTRAIT OF A VOLUNTEER

SEVENTEEN YEARS EARLIER, I was standing in a maze of cubicles on the ninth floor of the 550 Building on the east-Baltimore campus of Johns Hopkins Hospital. I was twenty-two years old, sandy blond, six feet tall, skinny, a few weeks removed from Amherst College, watching middle-aged men measure their rearranged cubicle spaces to see if they had lost or gained an inch.

I was in the public affairs office of the hospital, where I had worked each summer during college and was working again after graduation while I waited to hear back from the Peace Corps.

It was 1997, and "Mo' Money, Mo' Problems" by The Notorious B.I.G. was the song of the summer.

"Shit, I lost an inch," said Brian, on his hands and knees in a gray suit, holding a yellow measuring tape.

For some reason, Jeff was standing on his chair, measuring the top of a cubicle.

An older gentleman, a former reporter for *The Baltimore Sun*, slept at his desk. He had one of the smallest cubicles.

"You know, Ben," said Mike, the deputy manager, an employee with an actual office, walking up to me while I surveyed the aftermath of the Great Cubicle Rearrangement. "You'll always have a place here."

That's what I'm afraid of.

Later that day my phone rang.

"Good news," said the voice on the other end, an assistant to the African Country Director at Peace Corps headquarters in DC, "you're going to Namibia."

"Great," I said, matching his enthusiasm, wondering where Namibia was.

The Peace Corps handbook helpfully explained:

> The territory of Namibia is bordered on the north
> by Angola, on the east by the Republic of
> Botswana, and on the south-east and south by the
> Republic of South Africa . . . Namibia's climate is
> hot and dry.

Three months later, my parents were driving me from Baltimore to Washington, DC, dropping me off at the Washington Plaza Hotel, where my Peace Corps Namibia Group, Group 11, was staging.

About three blocks from the hotel, my dad, behind the wheel of our maroon Honda Accord, started pointing at different pedestrians.

"He's Peace Corps," said my dad. "She's Peace Corps."

A few minutes later, meeting the eighty-five members of Group 11, I saw he was correct.

From my journal:

> Peace Corps Volunteers have a certain look about
> them. Which is depressing because you think
> signing up for the Peace Corps you are doing this
> unique thing that stands out, only to find at

staging eighty-five other unique people just like you.

Two days later, having made the sixteen-hour flight over the cobalt-blue Atlantic Ocean to Johannesburg, South Africa, and then the two-hour flight over the rust-red Kalahari Desert, Group II touched down at Hosea Kutako International Airport in Windhoek, Namibia.

At twenty-two years old, I was one of the youngest in the group. On the bus ride from the airport to our hostel, I sat next to Deidre, a black-haired Chicagoan, also twenty-two.

"It's so dry," she said as we drove through Klein Windhoek, the wealthy suburb of Windhoek. The houses were more like fortresses, hidden behind walls and barbed wire. Lawns were dry yellow brush.

༄

Three months later, I was in a white Land Rover, the black tar road stretching ahead of us into infinity, trees and cattle rushing by.

"Engela," I said, half to myself.

"Eh?" asked Elon, the Peace Corps driver.

"Engela," I said again. It was the name of the village where I had been placed. With all those vowels, the name rolled off the tongue.

I'm going to the middle of nowhere in the middle of Africa to teach high school English.

Elon nodded. "Engela."

Engela was two miles from Angola, a country in the midst of a civil war. Every now and again, the sound of a stray shot drifted over the border like a lost soldier.

I lived with a local family. There was no electricity at the homestead, a collection of small huts and concrete structures. We fetched water in jugs from a tap in the yard. Sometimes, when the well was dry, the teenage girls who stayed in the house would walk a mile to the community tap and return with white plastic two-gallon buckets, filled with water, perfectly balanced on their heads as they walked across the worn dirt path through the mahangu wheat fields that led to the wooden gate of the homestead.

When it got dark there was no television to watch, no light by which to read. If I had grading to do I would use an oil lamp but that drew flies so, when the sun went down, I usually went to sleep. In the middle of the night I would use a flashlight, what the older folks in the village called an "electric torch," to find my way to the outhouse.

In the morning, when the sun came up and the rooster started crowing, I got out of bed, dressed, and walked two miles through dry, yellow grass to Engela Junior Secondary School, where I taught grades eight through ten.

In the center of the schoolyard was a full-length basketball court built by two previous volunteers.

When I was in middle school and high school I spent most of my free time in the library and always had a book cracked open on the bus ride home. When my younger sister joined the middle school basketball team my dad put up a hoop in our driveway so she could practice. For reasons unexplainable to me, except that the hoop was outside our door, I fell in love with the game, a deep, almost bottomless love. I practiced shot after shot, moving around the black tarmac of our driveway, sweating in the thick Baltimore heat.

I would tape NBA games and rewatch them, examining, for example, Hakeem Olajuwon's balletic footwork, rewinding the VHS tape over and over again and then go outside, practicing Olajuwon's "Dream Shake." I wasn't good enough to play on my high school team but I loved the feeling of getting better at the game.

In college at Amherst, my best friend Rey Harp and I played endless games together. Rey was the manager for the men's team and had a key to the gym. We would gather up a bunch of people from Drew House and have our own version of Midnight Madness. After college, while I was in the Peace Corps, Rey took a job as a history teacher at Northampton High School and, after a few years, became the boys basketball coach, leading the school to their first ever Western Mass title.

The team's name was the Blue Devils.

The basketball court at Engela Junior Secondary School was mostly used by the kids as a makeshift soccer pitch, but there it was, sitting in the middle of the schoolyard like an outdoor church. A few kids were interested in learning the game and sometimes after school or on the weekend I would teach the basics.

One day I was showing Kiki, the most athletic grade-ten student, how to make a layup.

"Can we practice again tomorrow?" he asked. Tomorrow was Saturday. No school.

"Sure," I said. "Meet here at ten."

"Yes, but you know, you white people," said Kiki. "You're always on time. We Namibians, we're not like that."

"True," I said, laughing. "Why is that?"

"Because when we're doing something, we're doing that thing. Not thinking about the next thing."

"Which way is better?" I asked.

Kiki smiled.

The next day Kiki was there with two of his brothers.

We shot around.

"You should start a team," said Kiki.

I didn't know anything about coaching.

"Maybe," I said, looking out over the empty space surrounding the school. "Who would we play?"

Kiki shrugged. "I don't know."

And then he added, "It's nice to be on a team."

"Let's play some two-on-two," I said.

The sounds of the game echoed across the empty school yard: the hollow sound of the ball bouncing, the thunk of the wooden backboard, the shh and squeak of sneakers on concrete, the clang of the rim, the slap of hands giving five, and the silence of a perfect shot swishing through the netless rim.

4

PORTRAIT OF THE COACH AS A YOUNG MAN

"BALL. YOU. MAN," said George Willis.

Mr. Willis, a Black man in his early fifties, with plenty of gray in his hair and a paunch that was slowly turning into a beach ball of a belly, still had the walk of the Division 1 athlete, basketball and baseball, that he'd been at Alcorn State in the early seventies.

After finishing Peace Corps in 1999, I joined the Mississippi Teacher Corps, a sort of Peace Corps for Mississippi. I had been placed in Hollandale, Mississippi, a town of about a thousand people in the heart of the Mississippi Delta. My school, Simmons High School, was bordered on both sides by cotton fields, row after row of perfectly straight snow-white shrubs, like soldiers standing at attention. For millennia, the flat land of the Mississippi Delta had received mineral-rich sediment draining from the Rocky Mountains. That alluvial plain formed the most fertile land on earth. The students I taught in Hollandale were the descendants of slaves. Some of their ancestors likely came from tribes who settled in what is now Namibia.

"Ball. You. Man," said Mr. Willis again.

It was the first day of practice, my first day as an assistant coach, as a coach of any kind, and Mr. Willis was demonstrating one of the game's fundamental defensive concepts—that an off-ball defender should always be between their man and the ball.

Mr. Willis was the winningest high school basketball coach in the state of Mississippi. He coached both the boys' and girls' teams, winning two state championships with the girls' team in the early nineties and a state championship with the boys' team back in 1975. Now, in 2000, Mr. Willis knew he had the chance for another title with the boys' team. We had a team of six seniors led by a chubby six-foot-six left-handed scorer named Jasper Johnson.

Our team name was the Blue Devils.

Mr. Willis had a way of correcting players' mistakes with criticism and humor in equal measure.

"The more you talk, the dumber I get," Mr. Willis said to Marcus Sanders, who was trying to explain why he had missed a defensive rotation.

When Jasper, our star player who could score from anywhere on the floor, missed a few shots, Mr. Willis said, "You couldn't hit a bull in the ass with a bull-ass-hitter."

Mr. Willis would yell at, embarrass, curse, and confront players. Having been a boxer growing up in Memphis, he had no problem with physical confrontation, but he also made the players laugh, lacing his hard truths with humor. It wasn't uncommon to walk into the gym and find Mr. Willis in a shooting contest with some of the players, or just random students, for money. They would play "Around the World," shooting threes at designated spots all the way around the three-point line and back. Mr. Willis, a former D-1 shooting guard, was a great shooter, and once the money was down, he would pick up a ball, look at his opponent, and say, "I'll see you when I get back."

Swish. Swish. Swish.

During games, he often walked the sidelines in a bright blue suit, a wedge of lemon stuck in his mouth as he sucked on the rind.

We made the state playoffs, and Jasper carried us to a championship. As the Simmons High School band performed in the stands of Jackson Coliseum, what everyone called "The Big House," I hugged Mr. Willis in his bright blue suit and said, "Twenty-five years. Twenty-five years."

Mr. Willis wiped the tears from his eyes.

A year later, I was offered the job of head varsity basketball coach at McLaurin Attendance Center in Star, Mississippi, a K–12 public school outside Jackson. The Principal and Assistant Principal said they were impressed by the gold championship ring I wore in the interview.

I accepted the job, thinking I had learned all I needed to learn in my two years as an assistant coach with Mr. Willis. I was twenty-seven and burning with competitiveness, but I wasn't experienced enough with the game or with life to be a good coach.

◈

"Focus! Or I will turn this practice into a fucking track meet," said Bob Knight, soon to be the NCAA's all-time winningest men's basketball coach, at one of his first practices as the new head coach of the Texas Tech Red Raiders. An interesting feature of American sports is that teams are often named after a group of people decimated by genocide. The Redskins. The Redmen. The Red Raiders.

A year earlier, Knight had been fired from Indiana University for various physical altercations with students, including choking one of his players. Instead of supporting the victims of Knight's violence, IU students rioted in protest when he was fired, and a year later, he was hired by Texas Tech, with their brand-new arena that housed 15,098 screaming fans.

Five hundred or so high school and middle school coaches sat in red plastic seats in one section of

United Spirit Arena, watching and listening to Knight, who was mic'd up, as he conducted practice.

I balanced a cold pastry on my knee and took notes. Knight wore khaki pants with an elastic, expandable waist. When one of the forwards made a mistake, Knight slapped him on the back of the head.

Later that afternoon, during the coaches-only session where Knight outlined his strategies on an overhead projector, he called over one of the team managers.

"So you got an earring this weekend?" said Knight, still mic'd up.

"Yes, sir," said the college student, nervous.

"You look like a girl," said Knight.

Five hundred high school coaches laughed.

"Get on the fucking line," said Mike Krzyzewski in his white Duke University polo, standing at the baseline of Cameron Indoor

Stadium in Durham, North Carolina. "You're playing like fucking idiots."

Fourteen young men, eighteen and nineteen-years-old, lined up on the opposite baseline. Krzyzewski blew his whistle and the players sprinted as hard as they could, running "suicides."

Raiders. Suicides. The language of sports is violence.

I was taking notes in my Duke University notebook. Duke and Coach K were the team and coach I had rooted for in high school and college.

"Fuck you," said Coach K to his players. "Fuck you if you don't want to play hard."

Coach K had played for Knight at Army and would succeed Knight as the all-time winningest men's basketball coach in NCAA history.

Like Knight, Krzyzewski was mic'd up for the benefit of the hundreds of high school coaches attending the coaching clinic.

"Tell the guys to be back here at midnight," he said to starting point guard Chris Duhon. Presumably, Krzyzewski was going to make the team run more suicides.

The winningest coaches in NCAA men's basketball history were about control and maintaining control through intimidation and insults, through curses and confrontation.

So was I.

🏀

" Concen-fucking-trate!" I said, standing on the top of the bleachers, to the teenagers below.

The McLaurin Tigers' Gym was painted green and gold. The hardwood floor had been finished with high-gloss polyurethane, and the smell was snapping at my nostrils when we started the first day of practice in August of 2002.

"Hot in Herre" had been the biggest song of the summer and I was already yelling at the players.

"On the fucking line," I said, standing high above the high schoolers who had come out for the team. "If you don't want to focus, I will turn this practice into a fucking track meet."

The young men stood at the yellow end line, dripping sweat, waiting for me to blow the whistle.

A fter one of our first practices at McLaurin, I gathered the players together and made a pronouncement.

"From now on, practice is about team strategy. Shooting and ballhandling, work on that at home."

I tried to install eight different defenses, from half-court man to full-court zone, overwhelming the high schoolers with information and neglecting the fundamentals. I didn't realize if players hadn't mastered the fundamentals, it didn't matter what offense or defense we ran.

I was an arrogant, useless coach, pretending to be a Mr. Willis or a Bob Knight or a Coach K, but in reality, I was lost, walking an unknown path with no map and no compass.

I stayed at McLaurin for one year. We finished 10 and 13, not a disaster, but the season was a failure. Twenty years later and the players I coached at McLaurin are now adults. I imagine there have been weddings and children, heartbreaks and triumphs. Some of them, perhaps, have gone on to become coaches themselves. I wouldn't know because I have no connection to any of them. I don't exchange text messages or DM's or Happy Birthday wishes on Facebook with anyone from that season.

At the end of the school year, I was offered a job at the University of Mississippi as Program Manager of the Mississippi Teacher Corps, the same program that had brought me to Mississippi.

I left McLaurin, and coaching basketball, behind.

5

EPIPHANY IN THE MISSISSIPPI DELTA

FOR MY JOB at the University of Mississippi, I often had to drive for hours to observe teachers in rural high schools. Mississippi is flat country, all cotton fields and catfish ponds. While I was driving through the Delta in my dark-blue University of Mississippi van, my thoughts often turned back to my time coaching at McLaurin.

In particular, I turned two experiences over and over again in my mind.

The first was that, in addition to coaching the varsity high school team, I was also the head coach for the middle school team. With the middle schoolers, my mindset was completely different. I viewed playing on the middle school team as skill development for the players. We had twenty kids. For each game, ten players "dressed" and everyone played equal minutes. We didn't win a game, but the kids had fun and improved at basketball. Although I hadn't recognized it at the time, there was a lesson there: basketball could be about learning the game and having fun with your teammates.

The second experience I turned over and over again in my mind came early in the varsity season when we played Brandon High School, a much bigger and better school. The game, Brandon's first of the season, was played in front of a packed crowd in their perfect box of a gym. They had scheduled us, a small 2A school, as a warm-up, an easy win before they began playing the larger 5A schools.

We probably won't win, so why not try something different?

There were other coaches to learn from, to model, besides Mr. Willis and Bob Knight and Mike Krzyzewski. I had been a fan of the Chicago Bulls of the 1990s and their coach, the "Zen Master," Phil Jackson. Jackson often let his players play, trusting them to work things out on the court.

In his book *Sacred Hoops*, Jackson wrote, "I wanted them to disconnect themselves from me, so they could connect with their teammates—and the game."

Facing off against Brandon High School, I decided not do any "coaching," or what I and the people in the stands considered coaching. I gave only a few instructions in the huddle before the tip, and after that, I forced myself to sit on the bench and not yell or call out plays. I let the players play, hardly moving for the rest of the game. Normally, I yelled out instructions, plays, and curses ("Concen-fucking-trate!"), all while walking back and forth along the sideline.

I didn't anticipate what would happen next. We kept the game close, and toward the end of the fourth quarter, we were up by two.

We've come this far. Let's see what happens.

With ten seconds left, Brandon High scored, tying the game.

My point guard looked at me: Did I want a timeout?

"Play," I mouthed silently, sitting on the bench, indicating with my hands that he should advance the ball.

The team came down and found our big man, Keith Brown, who had drifted out to the corner. He hit a three at the buzzer.

I sat on the bench, shocked. It was our biggest win of the season, an unexpected win against a much better team.

In his book *Eleven Rings*, Phil Jackson wrote, "The most we can hope for is to create the best possible conditions for success, then let go of the outcome . . . The soul of success is surrendering to what is."

Surrender to what is . . .

Like most competitive young coaches, I didn't learn from the experience. I didn't understand and did not yet trust my intuition. The next game, I was back to stalking the sidelines, yelling out plays and instructions. I was too impatient and egotistical. I wanted the team to win *because* of what I was doing, conducting the contest from the sideline rather than letting the game unfold as it was meant to.

Years later, I would read a quote from Eugen Herrigel's *Zen in the Art of Archery* that summed up my year at McLaurin:

What stands in your way is that you have a much too willful will. You think that what you do not do yourself does not happen.

I had been too willful, wanting to make something happen rather than surrendering to what is. Still, for that one game at Brandon High, I had gotten out of my own way, gotten out of my own ego, and something had worked.

There was a lesson buried there, if only I could uncover it.

Why was it that the less actively I coached, the better we played?

One Mississippi morning, as I drove through the Delta, the sky rose-red as day broke, a realization dawned on me.

When we try to impose our will, there is resistance. When we accept what is, there is peace.

I drove past catfish ponds, the surfaces still and smooth.

What did it matter? I was getting my PhD in Education. I would never coach again.

❧

I t was late summer in the year 2010, and Ron "Ronzo" Shapiro, with his long, graying hair, Tibetan prayer bead necklace, and faded blue jeans, was standing behind the bar of his juice shop, the Main Squeeze, a big wooden tree house of a building tucked behind a Pizza Hut in Oxford, Mississippi.

I was drinking a Velvet Elvis, a smoothie made up of peanut butter, banana, and honey.

Behind the bar, on two trays, rested several rows of young wheatgrass—emerald green, a magic, almost otherworldly green—which Ronzo used to make shots for his health-minded customers.

On this day, he was opining about how Oxford had become more and more corporate.

"If you win the rat race," he said, "you're still a rat."

I thought back to the maze of cubicles at Johns Hopkins.

2012. Atlanta, Georgia. I'd finished my PhD in Education and was consulting for the Southern Education Foundation, making more money than I had ever made before.

I had been back to visit Namibia twice. Life there was more present.

Which way is better?

One morning, I was walking to Gato Bitzco, my favorite breakfast spot in Candler Park, to get sweet potato pancakes when I noticed a sign in the doorway of the Kashi Yoga Studio offering a beginner's meditation class.

Two days later, I was sitting up straight in a hardback chair while the pleasantly plump Black woman leading the session instructed us to "take a deep breath in, take a deep breath out." The world, at least my anxious perception of the world, started to melt away, as if I was turning off a gas stove and watching the boiling water settle and then slowly calm.

Meditation is the most helpful thing I've done as an adult. The practice helps me stay present, stay in the moment, and accept what is.

When we try to impose our will, there is resistance. When we accept what is, there is peace.

A number of peer-reviewed studies have examined the benefits of meditation: greater attention span, reduced anxiety, and increased creativity, all elements of learning and performance. The impacts of meditation also include expanded awareness, kindness, and compassion. Meditate long enough and MRIs show that brain structure changes. The hippocampus, which controls learning and memory, grows in size, while the amygdala, the center of fear and anxiety, shrinks.

When I meditate, I focus on my breath and my mind starts to drift.

Sometimes I visualize myself and look down at my body, sitting cross-legged on my couch. My thoughts become less reactive, and the emotional volume turns down. Empathy and compassion radiate out, and I feel a connectedness to all people.

As children, we think we are the center of the universe, that if we stop living, the universe stops existing. As we grow older, our perception of others, our empathy, begins to widen. As our perception widens, so does our understanding of our own insignificance. The world doesn't care if we live or die. From this comes fear. Fear of loss, fear of suffering, fear of death.

In our fear and in our empathy, we can connect to others.

We know what it is to feel fear and to feel love, and in recognizing those truths, we recognize that we are joined together in suffering and joy on this little blue marble in this huge, empty universe.

Ball. You. Man.

We are linked cars on an endless subway line, all connected to each other. What do we transfer? Is it fear or is it love?

As I meditate, I breathe out the fear and breathe in the love.

I t was the spring of 2013, and I was deeply unhappy, with my job and with my life.

If you win the rat race . . .

Sitting alone in my apartment in Amherst, Massachusetts, I remembered that in Namibia, in the capital city of Windhoek, there had been a private, international high school. I looked them up on the web, sent them an email with my resume, and was on flight back to Namibia four weeks later, a two-year teaching contract in hand.

Which way is better?

It had been ten years since I taught high schoolers, and having changed and grown as a person, I decided to incorporate meditation into my teaching practice.

I began most of my English classes, grades eight through twelve, with five minutes of guided meditation. After the students came into class and sat down, I would say, "Okay, put everything down on your desk. Sit up straight. You may want to close your eyes. Now take a deep breath in through your nose and take a deep breath out through your mouth. As you breathe in, you feel your shoulders start to relax; you feel your back start to relax; you feel your body start to relax; and you feel your *mind* start to relax.

"As you breathe out," I continued, "you breathe out all of your stress, all of your worries, all of your fears."

The effect was immediate. The students, teenagers used to always being tethered to their devices, used to always being "on," calmed down. On the rare day when I didn't start class with meditation, there was a noticeable difference in focus and engagement.

This shit works.

The private, international school didn't offer any sports. One day, while I was talking to a senior from Angola whose mother worked in the oil industry, he mentioned that he played basketball for a local public school. The city championships, boys' and girls', were that weekend.

I hadn't thought about coaching in years, but I still loved watching the game and went to the city championships. I appreciated the way one of the girls' teams played team basketball, even though they lost. The team was from David Bezendhout High School. After the game, I approached the coach, Jacque, and told him I liked their teamwork and the way they played together. He invited me to come by practice, and soon, I was there every day in the off-season.

In Namibia, the school year runs from February to November. In January, Jacque said to me, "You know, the boys' team needs a coach . . ."

The current coach had been awarded a scholarship to study in Germany.

It's nice to be on a team.

I smiled. I thought my coaching days were long gone. Maybe they weren't.

Which way is better?

6

FIRST DAY OF PRACTICE

TALL WHEATGRASS, the adult version of the baby wheatgrass in Ronzo's juice shop, ringed the outdoor basketball court, keeping it partially hidden behind a wall of emerald green. To access the court, I parked in a lot at the top of a hill and waded through the waist-high grass to the court below.

Ten nervous young men stood before me.

I had carried my meditation practice to the classroom, and now, coaching again, I carried it to the basketball court. I asked them to sit down in a circle at center court.

"A warm shower feels good, right?" I asked, forgetting that half the guys probably took cold bucket baths. "Meditation is like a shower for your brain."

I then gave the instructions that I would repeat over and over again throughout the next two years.

"Close your eyes. Sit up straight. Take a deep breath in, a deep breath out . . ."

There were peeks from half-closed eyes and muffled laughs from the players. I didn't mind. Part of the practice of meditation is learning to let go of your ego.

"Deep breath in, deep breath out," I said, ten young Black men and one middle-aged white man with a metal whistle around his neck sitting at center court.

"Deep breath in, deep breath out."

We were sitting on a basketball court in Namibia, a country bordered by yellow desert and blue ocean.

"Deep breath in, deep breath out."

We were sitting on a basketball court in southern Africa, the cradle of life.

"Deep breath in, deep breath out."

We were sitting at center court on a tiny blue marble floating in infinite black space.

Ball. You. Man.

"When you're ready," I said, "open your eyes."

We were sitting quietly, smiling, reorienting to the world while the sun warmed us all.

"Okay," I said. "Let's practice."

We started our first drill, defensive slides. I demonstrated to the team what they should do, sliding backward diagonally across the green court of precut concrete blocks. They had been laid a tad unevenly, and every now and then, there was a slight lip where two mismatched blocks came together.

Slide, slide. Feet should never touch; legs should never cross.

It was the rainy season, which, in Namibia, doesn't mean rain, just a handful of clouds dotting the sky every afternoon like white brushstrokes on a blue canvas. I used children's sunscreen so the lotion wouldn't irritate my eyes when sweat ran down my face.

I watched the players go through the defensive slide drill. Mike had the most experience. He went first and did it reasonably well.

Sepo, maybe six foot two, was second. He had a gentle face and muscles that rippled down his arms, which were longer than most. He had been the first to arrive at practice. And every day for the next two years, Sepo would be the first player to arrive. Some days, I would find him doing defensive slides alone, holding a red brick in each hand.

Slide, slide.

Sepo finished and it was Vincent's turn. Vincent had a permanently sunny disposition, always smiling and slapping five with the others. Although it was clear he had never done this drill before, Vincent's athleticism prevented him from stumbling too badly.

All the guys on the team had played the previous season, but their coach, a local university student, didn't know much about team basketball and mostly let them play pick-up against each other during practice. The team had no understanding of the fundamentals of the game or how to play together as a team.

Jack, at six foot one, went next. He was quiet and unassuming. The only words Jack ever said to me that first year were "Yes, Coach" and "No, Coach," his Angolan Portuguese accent showing in the way he slurred the *s* at the end of *yes*. English was everyone's second language. Jack spoke Portuguese, and the rest of the guys spoke one of Namibia's eleven tribal languages, ranging from Oshiwambo to Silozi.

Halfway through the drill, Jack tripped, either from lack of coordination or from hitting one of those small lips on the court. He limped to the sideline, having strained something in his thigh.

It was the first drill of the first day of practice, and the players were so inexperienced, so uncoordinated, that one of them tripped, fell, and hurt himself on a simple defensive slide.

I sighed.

The wheatgrass swayed, unbothered by the novice basketball players or their coach, slowly bending and springing back.

What have I gotten myself into?

Deep breath in. Deep breath out.

PART II

Coaches overuse strategies that give them the illusion of control.

—Bill James

7

LEADERSHIP

TEEN BODIES HEAL QUICKLY, and Jack was ready to go next practice. His birthplace, Angola, the country on the northern border of Namibia, had been embroiled in a civil war for decades, ever since the end of Portuguese rule. One of the many destructive elements of colonization is that it teaches the oppressed to use the tools of the oppressor, the tools of violence and dehumanization, which then permeate through society.

Get on the fucking line.

In this way, violence and trauma are perpetuated down through generations.

Raiders. Suicides.

Angola was a petrostate. Politicians stayed in power through coercion and rigged elections, backed by Chevron and Exxon and BP, who all scooped up the vast amounts of oil possessed by the country. In the U.S. and Europe, these same oil companies preached clean energy and gave large donations to nonprofits, but in lesser-known regions of the world, they funded corrupt, authoritarian rulers.

Greed perpetuates greed. The need for more creates instability and violence. At the bottom of the pyramid, it is people like Jack who suffer.

Jack, his mother, two of his sisters, and three of his brothers, had fled Angola to make a better life in Namibia, the rare country in southern Africa that had a progressive democracy. They weren't *exactly* refugees, but they had left their home and everything they knew because of circumstances beyond their control.

Jack had an earnest look, observant eyes, and closely cropped hair. He wasn't the quickest to learn a new skill, but once Jack learned something, he did not forget.

Mike was the outspoken one. Cocky and flamboyant, he was always ready with a joke or a putdown for his teammates, his imitation diamond earring flashing in the sun. He was also the most accomplished player, the returning star from last season. Mike was used to taking shots whenever he wanted, and one of the things I would work on with him throughout the season was better shot selection. Still, in a close game, that kind of arrogance could come in handy. Mike might take an ill-advised shot, but he also had no qualms about taking a *big* shot.

Sepo was the leader, quiet and encouraging. An orphan, he had grown up in a small village in the far north of the country, working on neighboring farms for little pay. Life there was lived in thatched-roof huts and, during the rainy season, people had to travel in dugout canoes. To escape a future working on other people's farms to survive, Sepo moved to the capital city, Windhoek, and stayed with his uncle.

Sepo had a way of carrying himself that was confident and empathetic at the same time, an unusual combination for a teenager. The guys loved to be around him and looked for his approval.

Leadership is about lifting people up, not tearing them down. So often in sports we lionize the players and coaches who are difficult, who are tough on their teammates, who yell or scream or even punch their teammates. True leadership is often quiet and encouraging. It is the arm around the shoulder. Supportive. Present. Empathetic.

Sepo was all of those things.

In addition to his leadership skills, I noticed that Sepo could handle the ball well for a forward.

After watching Sepo practice for a few days and considering that he was always first to practice, I thought, maybe he could be our point guard. At six foot two, Sepo was tall for a point guard, but with the exception of Mike, none of the other players could handle the ball well enough to be our primary playmaker. And from a playmaking perspective, Mike's first option was usually Mike.

I asked Sepo to dribble two basketballs at the same time, a practice in education called "overloading" where you learn a new skill by practicing the skill under more extreme conditions than normally required. The idea is to overload the senses and speed up unconscious mastery. If Sepo could learn to dribble two balls consciously, he would be able to dribble one ball unconsciously. What was now difficult would become easy.

After two weeks of practice, Sepo was proficient at two-ball dribbling.

"Okay, now do it with three basketballs," I said.

"Coach . . ." said Sepo, squinting his eyes at me in disbelief.

"Try it," I said.

To make three-ball dribbling work, Sepo would have to throw one ball ahead while dribbling the other two and then catch up to the ball he had thrown ahead. It's like juggling, except instead of throwing three balls up in the air, Sepo would have to bounce three balls down on the court.

Bounce, bounce, throw.

"It's impossible," he said.

The thoughts we have about ourselves often become true. Those who think they can and those who think they can't are both usually correct.

"Try it," I said, smiling.

Sepo did and for the first two days, his attempts resembled a clown car of exploding basketballs. But on the third day, Sepo found the cadence of bounce, bounce, throw. By the end of the week, he was dribbling up and down the court with three balls. While he did this, the rest of the team would sometimes stop and stare.

It was settled, Sepo was our point guard.

Still, we had work to do. The players needed to learn the game. The style they knew was pick-up basketball, five players playing five different games of one-on-one at the same time and looking to the crowd for approval each time they scored. The players had no feel for the organic, connected nature of the team game, how spacing on one side of the court increased the team's scoring opportunity on the other side of the court. Their individual fundamentals consisted of slick dribbles and herky-jerky shooting motions. Scoring in basketball, whether a layup or a three pointer, is about being able to replicate the same motion with consistency. The guys were anything but consistent.

Years earlier, at McLaurin, I had expected players to work on the basics of the game during their free time. Practice, I told them, was for team offense and defense, not shooting and passing. This time I took a different approach. I was going to emphasize the fundamentals above all else.

I was going through the same experiences I had gone through at McLaurin but now as a different person. There is a circular path to life. We repeat the same actions with, hopefully, more knowledge and wisdom. It's how we learn. It's how we progress.

I was walking the same path, this time with a different stride.

8

FUNDAMENTALS

AFTER STARTING PRACTICE WITH MEDITATION, the guys would line up in rows, facing me. Without using a ball, we would, in slow motion, work through the various movements a player could make on the court.

From my years as a teacher and my PhD in Education, I had learned that one of the fundamental steps of skill acquisition is to first be able to perform each small component of a skill slowly, without stress, to encode the sequence in one's neural pathways. Once those fundamentals are mapped, a player can then begin to do them at speed.

The Navy SEALs have a saying: Slow is smooth. Smooth is fast.

We were starting with slow.

"V-cut," I said, demonstrating how each player should take two steps in one direction and then hard cut back the other way at an angle, making a *V*. This is the basic way a player gets open to receive a pass.

"V-cut," I said again. "V-cut," they said in unison, performing the action at half speed.

We moved onto the act of passing, again without a ball and in slow motion. Overhead pass. Fake one direction and pass to the other. Snap your hands and finish thumbs down. Focus on form. Next a chest pass. Step forward. Push out from your chest. Your teammate should give you a target directly beneath their chin. Now a bounce pass. Push down. Let your brain calculate the angle. Push hard. The ball should spring up.

For rebounding, I would mimic taking a shot, and the guys would yell, "Contest! Box out! Rebound!" going through all of those motions to get in position for a ball that was not there.

We would finish with shooting. Form a ninety-degree angle with your arm and forearm. Elbow in.

Push straight up. Hold the follow-through as if you were standing in front of a refrigerator, reaching up and into a cookie jar on top of the fridge.

No ball. Just form. Dip your hand in the jar.

I was putting into practice some of the theory I had learned during my PhD research. The field of study most interesting to me was how we learn, how we acquire a skill, and how we become proficient at that skill. The research is ever-growing but points in some fascinating directions, including that meditation helps super-charge learning, that focused repetition in slow motion grooves muscle memory, and that myelin, a substance that forms part of the white matter in our brain, is key.

Myelin is a powerful accelerant to performance. As the guys learned a new skill like the V-cut, or more correct ways of doing an old skill, like shooting, they were creating new neural pathways. At first, each of those pathways is slow, akin to driving on a bumpy, unpaved country road, and it takes a while for information to get from Point A to Point B. However, by practicing these skills slowly, without the distraction of live defense or even a ball, we were grooving new knowledge, smoothing out that country road and gaining speed. During this development and reinforcement process, the brain creates a fatty substance called myelin that sheathes the neural pathways. The fat from the myelin increases the rate of the electrical impulses that move from one nerve cell to the next. The thicker the myelin, the faster the connection. The more each player on the team grooved their knowledge, the thicker their myelin became, eventually transforming that country road into a superhighway. And with each repetition they were accelerating faster down the highway.

Each practice, after meditating, we worked the fundamentals in slow motion, with no ball, for about ten minutes.

Groove that knowledge.

After walking through the various motions that a player could make on the court, we added a ball and moved to layups. First, we practiced layups without dribbling. Hold the ball high and close to your chin. Step toward the basket. One, two, jump. Since players who can shoot layups from both sides are twice as effective, we practiced with both the right hand and the left hand.

From layups we moved to close shooting, standing one foot from the basket, shooting the ball with one arm and hand, concentrating on mechanics, keeping the elbow in, and holding the follow-through.

Dip your hand into the cookie jar.

When I filled out the paperwork for the high school league, the team didn't have a nickname, so I named them the Blue Devils. When I told the team about our name, Mike came up to me after practice, a concerned look on his face.

"Coach," he said, "I'm a Christian."

I explained that the name *Blue Devils* had no negative religious connotation, that it referred to a French commando unit in World War I that wore blue capes and berets and were nicknamed "les Diables Bleus." US troops took the name back to the States, and someone gave it to the Duke University athletic teams.

Mike nodded, but he looked skeptical.

9

TRUST

TRUST IS the most important factor in the performance of a high-functioning team. One of my failures at McLaurin was not building trust, which I define as psychological safety.

Psychological safety means a person can be vulnerable and not worry about being teased or ignored. The anti–Bob Knight philosophy.

Like myelin, building this type of trust takes time.

To the players, I was an alien from outer space—white, from another country, with no preexisting connection to any of them, to their families, or to anything with which they were familiar. The only authority I had was that Jacque, the girls' coach, had announced I was their new coach and, for the time being, they accepted that.

With each practice, I was putting in a few more hours and building up a few more degrees of trust.

We had ten players, and I knew all ten wanted to play. I thought back to my experience coaching the middle school team at McLaurin. When everyone played, the team collectively was joyful.

Of course, the middle school team hadn't won a game.

Was there a way to replicate that middle school joy in a competitive high school setting, a way to make playing on the team fun, build trust, and win games?

Through the grind of practice, always starting with meditation and then moving to the slow-motion grooving of the fundamentals, an idea formed: the Platoon System.

In the Platoon System, a coach subs out the entire team at a prearranged time, irrespective of who is playing well and who is playing poorly and regardless of the score. Five bench players would check in at the same time. Years before, I watched a girls' high school coach in Mississippi use the Platoon System to exhaust the opposing team. Ten players dressed, and everybody played. Five in, five out.

The Platoon System solved concerns over playing time as everyone played the same number of minutes. This would lead, I hoped, to everyone improving throughout the season and staying invested in the game even when they were on the bench. I also felt that the Platoon System solved some of the uncertainty and anxiety that bench players can feel from not knowing if and when they are going to play.

The downside to the Platoon System? The five best players on the team are *never* on the court at the same time; the idea is to mix stronger players with weaker players on each platoon. As a coach, that's both risky and frightening. There's a chance neither platoon will be effective. Or one group may play well, and the other may not. One may take a lead, and the other squander it. And, at the end of a close game, you would not have your best five on the floor.

There were so many reasons not to implement the Platoon System but I wouldn't know if it worked until I tried, and I was determined to try. I was doing things differently this time around the path.

Sepo and Mike were the two best players and the two best ball handlers. I decided Sepo would lead the first platoon and Mike would lead the second platoon. Five in, five out. I would start Sepo's group first, and then Mike would come off the bench.

"Coach," said Mike, approaching me after practice. "I'm a senior . . ."

He wanted to start. He was last year's star and had started every game.

"I know, Mike," I said, standing on the side as the guys shot around. "This is what is best for the team. You're going to play the same number of minutes whether you start or not."

Mike was focused on himself, on what he wanted, not on what was best for the team. His eyes glazed over as I explained my thinking.

I hadn't built up enough trust.

Yet.

10

THE TEST

OUR FIRST GAME of the season was against Khomas High School. Before the game, we set up some chairs at half-court and took our team photo. Sepo sat in the middle, the ball in his hands. It was the team's first time wearing their new jerseys, which I had ordered from South Africa. The jerseys had *BLUE DEVILS* printed on the front, with *BLUE* written above the number and *DEVILS* under it. Sepo chose #1.

"Blue Devils for life," said several players as they put the jerseys on, excited about their new uniforms.

I wasn't thinking about the jerseys; I was thinking about the game.

Were my ideas sound? Meditation, practicing the basics without a ball, the Platoon System . . . Would this shit really work?

Our opponent, Khomas High School, took the court to warm up, starting with a layup line. I had never seen them play. I had no film and no idea how good they might be. As they shot around, I studied their players, looking for an edge. I needn't have worried. They couldn't dribble well or finish left. Their shooting form was a mess, and their passes were slow.

They had not been practicing the fundamentals.

Once the game started, Khomas High couldn't stop us from scoring, and on defense, we hounded their ball handlers, creating turnover after turnover. After the first four minutes of the thirty-two-minute game, it was time to platoon. Sepo's team came out, and Mike's team went in, everyone high-fiving each other at the scorer's table. We continued to dominate. Throughout the game, each platoon cheered for the other, and we won by thirty points.

The players began to believe and, slowly, we were building trust.

Our next opponent was Augustineum, the big school on the block. They had two outstanding forwards, guys who were also playing in the Namibian professional league, the Khomas Basketball Association or KBA, while still seniors in high school. Unlike in the United States, players in Namibia could play in both the high school league and the professional league simultaneously, as long as they were eighteen or under. Sepo, for instance, was also a backup small forward for the Plaza Warriors, a team in the KBA. He hardly played, but someone had recognized his talent and signed him to the Warriors.

The level of play in the KBA was perhaps comparable to a Division III college league in the United States, while the level of high school play was a step down from a typical high school league in the U.S. In Namibia, there was a wider range of ability. The strongest players may have been able to play for just about any high school in the U.S., while the weakest might not have been able to keep up with a JV team.

Part of what I was attempting to do was bring all of the Blue Devils up to a certain level of competence. I noticed most coaches in Namibia coached the stars and left everyone else to fend for themselves. They

coached with anger and fear and intimidation, traditional "old school" coaching methods.

Concen-fucking-trate.

A method I had come to reject.

A team is going to be what it's going to be. I didn't
need to try to impose my will on it.

I was fine with being different, with focusing on the
bigger picture, which was building lasting relationships with players. That had been my biggest failure
at McLaurin and something I wanted to correct this
time around.

Basketball ends, but players will always remember
how you made them feel.

Winning our first game against Khomas High, a
weak opponent, was like the varsity team beating a
JV team. Facing Augustineum would be going up
against a college team. Unlike Sepo, the two big
players for Augustinuem played regular minutes
with their professional club.

We were still building trust and the team didn't yet
believe my unusual methods like the Platoon System
would work.

Augustineum would be the test.

The games at Augustineum were held in their multi-purpose hall, with a stage on one side of the court and balcony seating on the other, twenty feet up. Everything was wood: wooden floor, wooden stage, wooden balcony. A full-sized Namibian flag, green, red, and blue with a yellow sun in the corner, hung from the balcony.

Augustineum was a boarding school, so the dormitory kids, with nothing else to do on a Saturday, packed the stands, their legs draped over the side of the balcony. There were more kids on the stage behind the team benches, everyone yelling and screaming. Some adults brought giant drums and beat them for the entire game. Teenage boys walked around the court during the game, running across the baseline when the action was at the other end, showing off for the teenage girls huddled together in groups of three or four.

We meditated before the game, sitting in a circle on the outdoor court where we practiced, away from the chaos and noise in the gym.

The wheatgrass circling the court swayed in the warm breeze.

Once the game started, I ran the Platoon System, starting with Sepo's five and then subbing in Mike's five. Augustineum was a much better team than Khomas High, but we stayed with them, and the game was back and forth. In the fourth quarter, Mike hit back-to-back threes, holding his hand up after the ball swished through the net, showing off for the crowd. Mike's threes put us up by six points, a margin Augustineum could easily close.

Four minutes remained in the game.

As Mike had just hit back-to-back shots, most coaches would leave him in to see how far his hot streak could go. Instead, I subbed in Sepo's group, as the Platoon System dictated.

This was the moment. The Platoon System would work and I would earn more trust from the team, or it would fail and we would have to begin again.

As Mike came off the court, I made sure to slap five with him. I normally didn't do this but I wanted to demonstrate my encouragement. Our palms touched as Mike passed. He was giving the system, and me, a chance.

Sepo's squad played well, with everything revolving around and flowing from Sepo, who could rebound, pass, and score and who had the mindset and the leadership ability to share the ball with his teammates.

With a minute left, we were up by seven. Sepo got the rebound and passed ahead. One of our younger players made an open three.

We won by ten, beating Augustineum at Augustineum.

Afterward, the players and I gathered in the parking lot, huddled together in a circle. I looked around, taking in their smiling faces. They were shocked and happy. We were not supposed to have won.

I knew what they were thinking: *This shit works.*

I was thinking the same thing.

11

UNDEFEATED

LIKE A BULLET TRAIN the team rolled through the season undefeated. Not only did we go undefeated, we won every game by double digits. We were the kings of the high school league.

During this time I started listening to several local musicians and attending performances at The Warehouse, a theater space in the center of the city. My favorite Namibian artist was Shishani, whose music was like neo-soul African folk, a Namibian Lauryn Hill. Her album *Sessions in Poland* stayed in rotation in my car's CD player. The lyrics resonated with me.

"I let go, I let go of my expectations/'Cause now I know that everything changes . . ." she sang.

The team continued winning in the playoffs, making it all the way to the championship game against Shifidi High School.

Shifidi High was in a separate division, and we had not played each other during the regular season. They were also undefeated and had beaten Augustineum in the semi-finals.

The game was played at Augustineum because their gym had more seating and a stage for the television cameras to set up on. It was also one of the few indoor courts in the city.

As usual, the gym was packed: the kids in the balcony, the announcers and scorekeepers up on the stage, the television crew broadcasting the game to the nation, the referees standing off to the side, Angolan guys in tight jeans beating drums, barefoot boys blowing plastic vuvuzela horns, and people walking everywhere. It was the most chaotic atmosphere in which I had ever coached. It was just as crazy outside. After the game, I learned that only a few steps from the gym, one person was stabbed and two more robbed.

Vincent's mother was the only parent in the stands. She was the only parent to ever attend a game.

There were several games before ours, including the third-place game and the girls' championship game. We spent most of the run-up to our game in the open-air theater behind the gym. As the sun set behind us, we sat quietly on the warm stone tiers and meditated, the sounds of the game barely discernible.

I didn't give a big speech. We knew what we had to do and, by now, we were confident. From the way Sepo carried himself, with quiet purpose, I knew we would win. My only thought was, *Would we keep our streak intact and win by double digits?*

An official called us in as the girls' championship game was ending. Sepo led the way, walking in with focus and confidence. The rest of the team followed. As Sepo went, so went the team.

The two girls' teams were walking off the court as we entered, one group in tears and the other in triumph.

There were drawn out player introductions, and some waiting around for the television crew to get set. Our bench was in front of the stage where the scorekeeper and high school basketball officials sat. Behind them was a table laid out with the championship trophy, gold and silver medals for the players, and an award for High School Coach of the Year.

The Namibian national anthem played; the television crew gave the "Go" sign; and the game started.

Sepo hit three straight threes.

I knew he'd play well.

And then he picked up two fouls back-to-back.

In the first quarter.

In Namibia, in both the high school and the professional leagues, once a player reaches five fouls they are out of the game. This was the first time all season Sepo had gotten in foul trouble.

Should I pull him from the game or not?

I went back and forth. We were still running the Platoon System and it would disrupt the substitution pattern. Plus, Sepo was on fire.

But what if he picks up his third foul?

It was risky either way.

I left him in. Sepo immediately picked up his third foul.

Shit.

Now he had to sit for the rest of the first half.

I subbed Mike in for Sepo and then platooned around Mike.

Thanks to Sepo's hot start we were up nine at the end of the first quarter but, without him, our offense stopped flowing. The ball tended to stick rather than move quickly from player to player.

We were up six at halftime. Sepo came back in to start the third quarter but he was tentative and then picked up his fourth foul, the worst of both worlds.

I left Sepo in, but his confidence had waned. And with four fouls, all he could do on defense was watch as players drove past him.

We were up by three points with six minutes left in the game when Mike hit a three to put us back up by six.

After Mike hit his shot, the ball was knocked out of bounds and rolled through a hole in the wall underneath the balcony. There was no extra ball at the scorer's table, and the game paused while a young boy crawled through the hole to retrieve the ball. Shifidi High School's star player, Romeo, sat down on the court to rest. The other Shifidi players followed suit.

One of the benefits of the Platoon System was that the other team would tire and become demoralized every time they saw a fresh group of five players subbing in. As each second passed, with the Shifidi players sitting on the court, resting and catching their breath, I knew we were losing one of our most important advantages.

The boy finally emerged from the hole in the wall, the dark orange ball in his hands. The crowd cheered, and the game resumed. Romeo, now rested, found a comfortable rhythm and started hitting shot after shot for Shifidi.

Our lead was dwindling, and Sepo couldn't defend anyone for fear of fouling out. It felt like we were drowning, the waters closing in on us and no way to pull ourselves out. With less than a minute left, Romeo hit a shot to put Shifidi up by one.

When the horn sounded to end the game we had lost by four points.

So much for being undefeated, for winning every game by double digits.

Spectators streamed onto the court. The coaches for Shifidi hugged each other. The fans were dancing now, knowing this was the final game of the year. The wooden floor vibrated.

My players were in tears. We went outside to the parking lot and huddled up again. This time there was trust in what we were doing but shock and sadness in losing.

"You can do things the right way, and sometimes it doesn't work out," I said. "Part of life is understanding and accepting that."

Tears rolled down their faces, the winter wind ripping through us.

"What we want to happen and what does happen aren't always the same thing."

Life doesn't have Hollywood endings.

We were called inside to accept our second-place medals. They handed me the Coach of the Year trophy; the ballots had been cast before the game. I didn't feel like the Coach of the Year. I had made a critical mistake during the game by leaving Sepo in after he picked up his second foul. It was a judgement call, and I made the wrong one. Shifidi had gone undefeated and won the championship. The Coach of the Year trophy rightly belonged to their coach.

As the players stood with silver medals draped around their necks, I thought about the team. We had ten players. The five starters and Mike were seniors. This was the end of the road for them.

Or was it?

12

BLUE DEVILS FOR LIFE

THE CHAMPIONSHIP LOSS STUNG, but the season had been filled with camaraderie, connection, and joy. I didn't want those relationships to end. In the normal course of events, some of the six seniors would move on to university or work life, and a few, like Mike and Sepo, would sign with professional teams in the KBA.

I had a different idea.

I called Sepo, and we arranged to meet.

Sepo lived in Wanaheda, the central feature of which was the Wanaheda Police Station, a three-story red brick fortress with cells in the basement. Spreading out from the police station was a mix of housing, from proper one-story houses to homes that were falling apart. We weren't far enough out from the city to be in tin shack territory, but they were only minutes away.

Wanaheda was old Windhoek. Black folks had been forced to live there for a long time. Even though apartheid was decades past, the scar tissue remained.

Driving to meet Sepo, I listened to Shishani's *Sessions in Poland* CD. "Everybody needs to lose in order to find . . ." she sang.

If that wasn't the truth.

Sepo and I met in an empty parking lot opposite the police station, two blocks from Sepo's uncle's house. I told him I was thinking of starting a professional team in the Khomas Basketball Association, but I first wanted to gauge his interest. If he wasn't interested in playing, the rest of the guys would not be either.

As Sepo went, so went the team.

Sepo played for the KBA's Plaza Warriors, an established club with veteran players, money, and history of winning, only two years removed from a championship. I was proposing to create a team from scratch, the Blue Devils Basketball Club, with no history and no money to pay anyone. The KBA was recognized internationally as a professional league, but the reality was different. Even though most clubs paid their players something, and the biggest stars commanded about $500 a month, some clubs connected to universities didn't pay their players at all. Sepo's team, the Plaza Warriors, was one of the more established clubs. Because he was so young and didn't play much, Sepo had not been paid by the Warriors. But they were a popular club, and Sepo gained status just by being a member of the team. Leaving the Warriors to play for nothing for a team that did not yet exist was a big ask.

Sepo sat quietly in the passenger seat of my car and listened as I explained my idea of a Blue Devils Basketball Club. Shishani's *Sessions in Poland* played quietly in the background.

"What do you think?" I asked.

Sepo smiled, every bit the quiet, confident leader.

"Blue Devils for life," he said.

PART III

A skilled craftsman leaves no traces.

—Lao-Tzu

13

BIG LEAGUES

IN NAMIBIA, the KBA was the big leagues. Some of the players had played professionally overseas in Europe and in South Africa's pro league, the best on the continent.

Even for Sepo and Mike, our two top players, playing in the KBA would be challenging. Mike said that in order to play, he would have to travel back and forth from Windhoek to the coastal town of Luderitz, about eight hours away, where he planned to live with his mother after high school.

We needed more players.

Sepo recruited a sharpshooting college student named Penda who he knew from pickup games in the city. Penda was model handsome, hardworking, and hoped to go to medical school. He had never played for an organized team before, but the form on his jumper was diamond smooth. Over the course of the season Penda would become a formidable shooter.

Another recent high school graduate, Mevin, had moved to Windhoek for university. The team and I had met Mevin the previous year when the Blue Devils scrimmaged against the Under-17 National Team. Mevin was the best player on the U-17 team, a lithe center who could defend every position on the court, score easily around the basket, and gobble up rebounds. He was tall, maybe six foot five, with a long face and dreads just growing out. He had dyed the tips of his dreadlocks light brown, a popular style at the time.

Mevin was Caprivian, a tribe far to the northeast in an area on the Caprivi River where, like Sepo, he had grown up traveling by canoe during the rainy season. Sepo and Mevin became fast friends and, as the two superstars, formed the cornerstone of our team. Sepo would be the playmaker and vocal wing defender, while Mevin, a quick and agile center, would hold down the middle as a shot blocker and rebounder who could also finish close to the basket.

Mevin was quiet and reserved around me. I suspected it had to do with my skin color and the well-deserved distrust that some Black Namibians have for white people after living under apartheid for decades. Even though Mevin and the rest of the team had not yet been born when Namibia achieved her independence, the deep cultural and historical wounds, the trauma of apartheid, remained. Trauma perpetuates trauma. For most of the players I was the first white person with whom they had spent any significant amount of time.

Munya, a friend of Mevin's who had already played several seasons in the KBA, also joined our team and became our starting small forward. Munya, in his mid-twenties and more experienced than the others, became my de facto assistant coach. All our players were muscular, but even amid this athletic group, Munya stood out. His body fat was nonexistent, and on his dark skin, even at rest, every muscle shone through.

Like Sepo and Mevin, Munya was a Caprivian, and he knew Mevin from their home village. They lived together in a flophouse in Windhoek.

Jack and Vincent joined us from the high school team and, as juniors, would play in both the high school league and the KBA. Jack still rarely said anything more than "Yes, Coach" and "No, Coach" to me, but I remained impressed by his diligence and demeanor. He never got too up or too down, and his quietness masked a deep understanding of the game. Jack's brain was like a computer processor. While he wasn't the fastest player in the world, his near-instant recognition of what was happening made him quicker than he seemed.

Vincent, a shooting guard who couldn't shoot, was the ultimate end-of-the-bench player, always smiling and slapping five. He brought guys together and was unconcerned with playing time. His joy came from seeing the guys, his friends, play well. Although his mother hailed from Kenya, Vincent had been born in Namibia and was a city kid, having grown up in Windhoek.

We added two more high schoolers, Sammy and Alonzo, to fill out the end of the bench. Stan, a

fifteen-year-old Angolan who burst with enthusiasm, was our manager/cameraman. When Mike was
available, we were nine strong. Except for Munya,
the rest of the team either was in high school or had
graduated only a few months earlier.

During preseason, our routine remained the same as
it had been in high school. Meditate. Practice, first
without the ball, then with the ball. Get better each
day. Groove that knowledge and build up that
myelin. By the start of our season, these routines
were so ingrained with my veteran players that the
new ones immediately fell into the rhythm of our
strange practices. The culture had been set in the
previous year, and now anyone who joined the team
adapted.

I preached steady improvement to the team at practice, and our goal was to make the playoffs. That
would be an outstanding accomplishment for a team
of teenagers.

With only nine players, however, I could no longer
use the Platoon System. It had served its purpose,
building trust and giving everyone an incentive to
improve, but now, in the big leagues, the best players
would play the majority of the minutes. That meant

that Vincent would not play much. His shooting and ballhandling were too unreliable. He didn't complain or sulk; he just continued to work hard and cheer on his teammates.

There were eight teams in the league. Each team played each other twice, making for a fourteen-game regular season. Games in the KBA were forty minutes long with four ten-minute quarters, as opposed to thirty-two minutes in high school. And at the end of the season, the top four teams made the playoffs. Since Mevin and Sepo were our two best players, I built our rotations around them, usually sitting Mevin at the end of the first and third quarters and Sepo at the start of the second and fourth quarters.

With our discipline and young legs, we got off to an impressive start. We won our first two games as Mevin and Sepo dominated their positions, point guard and center, running pick and roll after pick and roll or what we called "Number One." Most players on other teams played to the crowd, trying high-risk passes and low-percentage threes. We stayed focused on the basics, faking a pass before making a pass, driving right or left, and taking high-percentage shots. I designated the areas on the court from where we should shoot threes and layups and then charted each game according to the quality of the shot we attempted, not whether the shot went in.

Munya, like most KBA veterans, loved to show off for the fans. Seeking attention from the crowd indicated that he wasn't staying present in the moment, nor was he staying connected to his teammates. He was seeking outside approval. I wanted us to be detached, both from the crowd and from the outcome, and I wanted us connected only to each other.

"Pretend a curtain has dropped in front of the crowd," I said. "The only place you should look is our bench."

Munya nodded but still peeked at the crowd from time to time.

During the season, I held Sunday barbecues to build camaraderie. I had a Nintendo Wii, and the team held dance-offs and Mario Kart races. I posted some photos of the barbecues on Facebook and tagged the players. Deidre, the Peace Corps Volunteer who sat next to me on the bus eighteen years earlier as we drove into Windhoek, reached out when she saw the photos. Like me, during her volunteer service, she had lived with a family in a village, and Penda, our model-handsome shooter, had been a small child at her homestead. Penda's family had referred to Deidre as their American daughter, and Penda was her homestead brother. Penda's face lit up when I mentioned Deidre, a nice reminder that, however improbably, we are all connected.

During the season, Jack continued to improve. He didn't wow the crowd with two-handed dunks or behind-the-back passes; his best skill was his decision-making. He almost never turned the ball over, and he scored efficiently with floaters and put-backs, able to finish with either hand. Not making mistakes is a talent that is difficult to discern because it is the *absence* of something. Most KBA fans didn't recognize that Jack was the one who floated to the corner to keep the lane open or the one who kept the ball moving from teammate to teammate.

As a player, he was like a sheath of myelin, connecting everyone with his quick decisions and passes, accelerating the team's offense. On defense, Jack seemed to anticipate what was going to happen before it happened, often getting steals and deflections from being in the right place at the right time.

His play was so subtle that I often only recognized his full contributions later, when I watched video of the game, running the plays back in slow motion on my laptop.

After starting the season with two wins, we lost two straight. That's how it went for the year, back and forth as our record hovered around .500. To keep the team focused, I leaned on meditation even more.

"We don't get too high when we win, and we don't get too low when we lose," I said as we sat together in the center circle of Augustineum's outdoor court, the light green concrete blocks toasty warm.

"Stay even. Stay present. Stay in the moment."

As with our basketball skills, we grooved this philosophy of detachment from the outcome.

My coaching approach evolved as well. We practiced the fundamentals every day, but now, with a year's worth of development and trust built up, we spent more time on team concepts like spacing and defense. In practice, I gave near-constant instructions and correction, writing out my practice plans to the minute, but in games, I removed myself even more, often calling timeouts and then directing one player, usually Sepo, to conduct the huddle. The first few times I did this, I stayed in the huddle, listening, but after a few games, I would simply call timeout, say "Sepo, you talk," and then go back to my coach's seat, trusting the players to trust themselves, trust their intuition, and trust each other. My job was to sit on the bench and watch, like that game all those years ago against Brandon High School. I sometimes thought of this approach as "anti-coaching" because it looked so different from what we think of as traditional coaching.

When we try to impose our will, there is resistance. When we accept what is, there is peace.

At halftime, I would walk slowly to halfcourt, alone, and stand there, hand on my chin, thinking about what I had observed in the first half. I would come up with three or four adjustments and then narrow those adjustments to the single most important one. With one minute left, I would call a huddle and repeat the one adjustment over and over again. "Box out," or "Pass fake," or "Talk more." One adjustment, repeated over and over again. When I finished, I would ask each of the players to repeat it out loud.

I was making the complex simple, doing more coaching and less coaching at the same time.

In our second season together, Sepo and I became simpatico. Often, as I was thinking, "Run Number One here," Sepo would call for a pick and roll. Teamed up with the perfect partner in Mevin, Sepo played with pure joy. When one of his teammates scored a big basket, he would drop two fingers in a downward motion, signifying "count it."

As we slowly added more complexity to our offense, I signed up for an email newsletter published by a basketball coach from the University of Maine. One of the first emails I received included a link to a side-line-out-of-bounds play used by the Boston Celtics. I taught the deceptively simple play to the team.

At the end of a close game, when inbounding the ball from the sideline in front of our own basket, and with the opposing defense closely guarding us in hope of making a steal, three of our players would bunch up at the top of the three-point line while a fourth player, Mevin, waited in the backcourt.

Once the inbounder, usually Sepo, slapped the ball, two of the three bunched up players would break to either side of the court, to the wings, hands ready to catch and shoot a three-pointer. They were the decoys. The third player, the one who remained at the top of the three-point line, would turn and set a pick on the defender guarding our player in the backcourt.

The player in the backcourt, Mevin, would then run straight toward our basket. As his teammate at the top of the three-point line picked off his defender, Mevin would, in theory, be wide open for a layup.

The tricky thing about the play is that, in basketball, a player has only five seconds to inbound the ball. The referee, after handing the ball to the inbounder, would begin to count off the five seconds by extending his right arm to indicate each passing second. Because this play was designed to work off of the misdirection of the two players cutting to the opposite wings, and because our player in the backcourt had to wait for that action to unfold before he could start his run, five seconds could easily be exhausted before we inbounded the ball. We worked on the timing in practice, but it was always close. A strict referee might call a five-second violation.

I named the play "Boston" after the team that origi-
nated it, and we rehearsed Boston a few times every
practice with every configuration of players
throughout the entire season. It was a play that was
designed for a very particular end-of-game situation,
one in which we were up by a few points and the
other team would defend each of our players closely
in hopes of getting a steal.

O f the eight teams in the league, the Wolves
were the favorites to win the championship.
They were financed by a Chinese businessman
named Sky who loved basketball and had money to
throw around. He bought the best player in the
league, Allan, a do-it-all Swiss Army Knife on the
court. The Wolves also had the best center in the
league, Paulo, a wiry tough guy who moonlighted as
a collector for a loan shark. Although intimidating
and missing his two front teeth, Paulo had a kind
smile to go along with a killer post-up game.

The other players and coaches in the KBA knew
about our practice of meditation. Allan, the alpha
male of the league, the Most Valuable Player, would

walk into the gym, see us warming up, and taunt us, yelling out "Deep breath in, deep breath out!" or "Stay in the moment!"

I didn't mind that he was trying to gain a psychological edge. One of the benefits of meditation is that the volume of your ego turns down. I was pleased to be known as the coach who meditated.

The Wolves held first place in the standings throughout the season. They beat us twice, by more than twenty points each time.

The University of Namibia Pacers, coached by perhaps the best coach in Namibia, a tall Zimbabwean named Mpume, finished second. Like us, the Pacers were deep, with Mpume regularly fielding ten players. The Pacers were led by Mike Mukuya, a smart, scrappy forward nicknamed "Starter Pack" because of his potential.

The third-place team was the Barleys, a bunch of KBA lifers who got by on smarts and teamwork. While the Wolves enjoyed first place, the Pacers second, and the Barleys third, we fought it out with the Polytechnic Blues for fourth place, both of us trying to make the playoffs.

Although Poly and Blue Devils finished the season with identical records and had split our season series, we made the playoffs though the tiebreaker, which was our head-to-head point differential. We had lost to Poly by three points at the beginning of the season but had beaten them by four points toward the end of the season. That one point made all the difference. We had made the playoffs.

Of course, that meant that as the fourth seed, we would have to face the Wolves in the first round. Still, we had achieved our goal from preseason and had a week to practice before the playoffs began.

After our final regular season game, the guys went out to celebrate, and I went home to sleep.

Sepo called me first thing in the morning.

"Coach," he said, "I'm in jail."

14

SEPO

"WHAT HAPPENED?" I asked, in that space after *some-thing* has happened and all you can do is wait for more information.

"I got a DUI," said Sepo.

After our final game, Sepo had borrowed his uncle's car, and he and a couple of players went for beers. Sepo's uncle lived near the Wanaheda Police Station. Driving home, a block from the house, he was stopped at a roadblock. Sepo failed his DUI and spent the night in jail.

The next morning, an officer had given Sepo his cell phone and told him he could make one phone call. Sepo called me.

Fortunately, my friend Dennis was a former police officer. We went down to the station together. Dennis talked to the desk sergeant and arranged for Sepo to be released.

Sepo looked like someone who'd spent the night in jail. No sleep. Smelled of alcohol and fear. I walked him to his car. He was only nineteen-years-old, his whole life ahead of him.

"You made a mistake," I said. "Go home and get some rest."

"What about practice?" Sepo asked. It was Saturday, and we had practice that afternoon.

"No practice for you today," I said. "Get cleaned up and get some sleep. Practice tomorrow." In preparation for the playoffs we were practicing every day.

Sepo nodded. I hugged him, this young man who was an orphan, who had no one in his life to guide him, whose first phone call from jail was to his basketball coach.

"You made a mistake, but you're not a bad person," I said. "I love you and I care about you."

I wanted Sepo to understand that what he had done was wrong *and* that I cared about him. I didn't want to fill him with shame or fear. I wanted him to know that one mistake didn't define him. The universe had treated him with indifference. I wanted Sepo to know he mattered and he was loved.

We are all connected.

"Thank you," said Sepo. He got in his uncle's car and drove away.

"I hope he's going to be okay," I said.

"He'll go home and get some rest,' said Dennis.

"No, I mean I hope he's going to be *okay*," I said.

Dennis shrugged. He was Namibian. Life had dealt Sepo nothing but spot cards. Dennis had seen that hand played many times before. It usually didn't end well.

Life doesn't have Hollywood endings.

I drove to practice, not explaining to the guys why Sepo was absent. Jack had been working on his ball-handling and was turning into an outstanding over-sized point guard. I had often thought that of all the players I coached, Jack and Sepo would be coaches one day. I smiled as I watched Jack do two-ball and three-ball dribbling, the same drills Sepo had done the year before.

Sounds of soccer drifted over us. The wheatgrass swayed in silence.

Sepo came back to practice the next day, ready to go.

T he playoffs were two rounds, best of three each round. To move on, we would have to beat the Wolves twice. Our two regular season games hadn't been close, but we had been steadily improving, and the time we spent on fundamentals was paying off.

In preparation for the playoffs, we continued to practice Boston, our special sideline-out-of-bounds play. At this point in the season, never having run the play in a game, it was as much a routine as anything else.

Before game one against the Wolves, Allan, the best player on the Wolves, and I were invited to appear on national radio to discuss the matchup.

Allan, who had played professionally in Germany, said the Blue Devils were an up-and-coming team, a well-coached team, but he made it clear we wouldn't pose a challenge to the Wolves.

Over the radio waves, I said, "The Wolves are a great team. They are the favorites. But we are not here to roll over. We are here to compete."

The host asked us for our predictions.

"I think we're going to win by twenty," said Allan, confident, as he should've been.

"And your prediction?" asked the host, looking at me.

"To be continued," I said.

15

COACHING PHILOSOPHY

THE WOLVES *WERE* the better team. They had Allan, a do-it-all wing player in his absolute prime. And they had Paulo, their tough center. Complementing those two local superstars, they had a bunch of outstanding shooters and role-players, mostly Chinese nationals hired by Sky.

Allan and Sky had started the team from scratch, poaching players from other teams. And Sky wasn't just the bankroll, he was the starting point guard. The team was a way of fulfilling his dream of playing professional basketball. However, his ego was a little bit bigger than his skill set, and he was both the weakest link on the starting five and the smallest player. I decided to put Mevin, six foot five and athletic, on Sky to disrupt their offense. By putting our quickest and best interior defender on Sky, Mevin was free to roam and make plays from everywhere. On one play, he might pick up Sky full court; on another, he might leave Sky completely alone and clog up the lane, helping Munya who was tasked with guarding Paulo, giving up several inches and thirty or so pounds.

Sepo, on the other hand, would guard Allan. I was asking a lot of Sepo: run the offense, lead the team, and guard the best player in the league.

Usually, I was nervous before the start of a game, wanting us to play well, but no matter the opponent, once the game started, my nerves dissipated. After tip-off, ninety percent of my coaching was done, and much of my role was only to remind the players of what we had already practiced.

"Get back."

"Box out."

"Run Number One."

That was it. On the bench during a game, I was one step above a fast-food cashier calling in orders.

"Big Mac. Extra pickles. Vanilla Coke."

By the time the game entered the fourth quarter, I was completely calm. Ninety-nine percent of my coaching was done. What was going to happen was going to happen.

During competition, I now saw my goal as a coach to release pressure, lower stress levels, and stay out of the way—that's it. We perform at our best when we feel prepared and relaxed. Many coaches had missed that lesson.

Which way is better?

Other than keeping two timeouts, at the start of the fourth quarter, my job was done. The real work had already been completed on the practice court. In the game, I felt like a craps player who, having thrown the dice, waited to see what number came up. I was no longer the coach I had been at McLaurin, burning with competitiveness, trying to conduct an outcome from the sidelines.

I had changed.

I had learned.

Coaching middle school at McLaurin taught me that playing basketball as part of a team should be a joyous experience. Coaching high school at McLaurin taught me to focus on relationships, not wins and losses. Studying education taught me to focus on the process of learning, not the outcome. Meditation taught me to stay in the moment.

All of these lessons would come together in the playoffs.

PART IV

Shall I be able to manage it? Wait patiently, and see what comes . . .

—Eugen Herrigel, *Zen in the Art of Archery*

16

GAME ONE

It WAS Friday evening and the stands at Gym Hall were filled with people drinking from red plastic cups and metal flasks. The KBA community was there to have a good time and watch the Wolves destroy the Blue Devils in game one of the semi-finals.

Sepo and Mevin started the game by running the pick and roll to perfection, scoring layup after layup. The Wolves adjusted, sagging in on defense and leaving Penda, our model-handsome shooter, wide open. Penda responded by hitting five threes in the first half. Mike came off the bench with his typical moxie, betraying no nerves about playing in such a big game. Vincent, as usual, cheered the team on from the bench.

We were rolling, but there was a problem: Sepo picked up two fouls in the first half, the second about halfway through the second quarter. Learning my lesson from last year's high school championship, I pulled him from the game.

Sepo sat for the rest of the first half, and we held on without him. At the start of the third quarter, I put Sepo back in and. for eight minutes, he played perfect basketball. He hit three three-pointers, made a three-point play, and scored two layups. Sixteen points in eight minutes.

Even though Sepo was scoring, he was not playing selfishly. He handled the ball, called out our plays, passed well, rebounded, and defended Allan.

We were up by eighteen points, all connected to Sepo's dominance in every aspect of the game, and then he picked up his third foul with two minutes left in the third quarter. I sent Vincent in to the scorer's table to replace Sepo until the start of the fourth quarter.

Vincent was sitting there, waiting to go in, when Sepo picked up his fourth foul.

Shit.

Now that Sepo had four fouls, I knew I was going to have to sit him longer than I wanted to in the fourth quarter.

Sepo came out and Vincent went in.

The Wolves chipped away at our lead. Allan would get a rebound and, without Sepo guarding him, dribble the length of the court and finish at the rim. He had two three-point plays at the end of the third quarter. By the time the fourth quarter started, our lead was six points.

Down from eighteen.

How long could we go without Sepo?

FOURTH QUARTER

Sepo started the fourth quarter on the bench, and without our primary defender on Allan, the Wolves kept scoring.

Finally, with 7:45 on the clock, clinging to a two-point lead, I sent Sepo back in.

Right away, Sepo got the team set up in our offense and passed the ball to Mevin, who was fouled. Mevin hit two free throws, and we were back up by four. And then Sepo committed his fifth foul.

He had played all of forty-five seconds in the fourth quarter before fouling out.

I glanced at the clock.

Seven minutes left.

Mike, our sixth man and backup point guard, went in with the rest of the starters. Vincent, slapping five and encouraging everyone, was on the bench. He knew he wouldn't play in the fourth quarter, not in a game like this.

The Wolves scored again and again, bringing up memories of the high school championship against Shifidi. The waters from last year were closing in on us. History was repeating itself.

Stay in the moment.

With three minutes left, the Wolves were up by five points.

Mike was fouled and made two free throws. We were down three.

And then Mike fouled out.

Two minutes left, down three, and now both our starting point guard and our backup point guard had fouled out.

I took a timeout.

"Vincent, you're in," I said. This was his moment. Ready or not.

"Yes, Coach."

No hesitation. Good.

I looked at Mevin, our center and all-around best remaining player, and said, "You handle the ball. You bring it up."

Mevin nodded. I had no idea if it would work.

Munya, muscles glistening, was locked in. He had sacrificed his body to guard Paulo, the best center in the league. After the game, Munya would be so sore he could barely move.

I looked at Penda and Vincent, telling them both the same thing, "Catch and shoot."

Penda was a great shooter. Vincent was not. But I didn't want either of them second-guessing their shot. I repeated what I said, looking back and forth at both of them.

"Catch and shoot," I repeated.

They both nodded, fully engaged.

The whistle blew. Two minutes left. Down three.

Vincent walked onto the court with Mevin, Jack, Munya, and Penda.

All decisions had been made.

18

VINCENT

MEVIN, handling the ball as I asked, came down and scored a layup.

One point game. A minute and fifty seconds left.

I was completely calm. I had one timeout left, saved, if needed, for the final seconds of the game. Other than that, I didn't need to do a thing. The game was going to be decided by the players on the court.

We were down one.

Paulo, the Wolves' star center, scored on a tough layup.

Wolves up three.

A minute and forty seconds left.

We missed a three. The Wolves came down and tried to set up their offense, but Penda got a steal and passed the ball ahead to Vincent.

Eighty seconds left.

The crowd was *screaming*. No one expected the game to be this close.

Vincent dribbled up the court, attacked the basket, then pulled back behind the three-point line, and let it fly.

Swish.

Tie game.

Vincent, all of seventeen-years-old, the second to last guy on the bench, only in because Sepo and Mike fouled out, had scored the game-tying three with seventy seconds left.

The Wolves came back and went to Paulo. Paulo hit a layup and was fouled. He made the free throw.

Wolves up three with sixty seconds left.

Mevin handled the ball again and passed to Munya, who drove and kicked it to Vincent at the three-point line.

Vincent didn't hesitate. Catch and shoot. Swish.

Tie game.

Fifty seconds left.

Sepo and Mike, on the bench, cheered for Vincent.

The Wolves brought the ball down and passed it around, tentative.

Thirty seconds left.

The Wolves airballed a three, their nerves getting to them. Jack got the rebound and passed to Mevin.

Twenty seconds left.

Mevin brought the ball up and handed off to Vincent.

Fifteen seconds.

Vincent, in the moment, didn't hesitate. He took the handoff, turned the corner, drove to the basket, and shot a contested ten-foot runner.

Nothing but net.

We were up two.

Vincent had scored eight points in sixty seconds.

Vincent!

Twelve seconds remained.

The Wolves inbounded the ball.Munya took a charge from Paulo at half-court, sacrificing his body one last time for the team.

Turnover Wolves.

Five seconds left.

We quickly inbounded and ran out the clock.

Game Blue Devils.

Now the crowd was yelling and cheering and heckling the Wolves. People couldn't believe what they had just seen.

We streamed out into the warm spring air and huddled up, the guys smiling in happiness and disbelief.

"Vincent is the first one off the bench to cheer for you. And tonight . . . tonight he won the game for you," I said.

The team high-fived and hugged Vincent.

He had hit two threes and a contested runner in the final minute of the game. The next day, at the end of practice, I asked Vincent to recreate the three shots he had hit. With no defenders on him and without the pressure of a playoff game, Vincent missed all three shots.

The team, Vincent, and I all dissolved into laughter.

19

GAME TWO

THERE WAS a ten-day break between game one and game two.

I didn't think anyone expected us to win game two. If people were being charitable, they probably thought that the Wolves would blow us out in game two, and we *might* have a puncher's chance in game three. My hope was that we could weather the first quarter and then give ourselves an opportunity to win.

At our last practice before the game, I talked to the team about how research showed a link between sleep and improved athletic performance.

When I picked the team up at 4:00 p.m. the next day, Sepo was yawning.

"I just woke up from a nap," he said.

Mike, Sepo, Jack, and Vincent rode with me. We had been together since that first day on the outdoor court when I had taught them meditation and when Jack had tripped and hurt himself. I called them my "Day One" guys.

In the week leading up to game two, Mike was supposed to go to Luderitz, on the coast, to stay with his mom, but Mike knew that if he was home, his mom might not let him come back to Windhoek for the game. He conveniently missed the bus two days in a row.

As we drove to UNAM, I played Shishani's *Sessions in Poland* album, her songs helping to create a relaxed, meditative state.

"I just want to put my feet in the sand/And turn around circles in an endless dance/Let the wind blow me away . . ." she sang.

We turned into the University of Namibia, imagining sand and beaches and the wind blowing us away. A line of cars was parked outside Gym Hall. In front of the entrance, Allan's light blue Audi was parked next to Sky's white BMW.

The stands were packed. A DJ was set up in the corner, spinning digital records. The scent of popcorn and grilled sausage from concessions floated in the air. Older fans snuck beer and flasks with "hot stuff" into the gym. Longtime fans and retired players who hadn't been at a game in ages turned up. Everyone who was anyone in the world of Namibian basketball was there.

The game started and I took my seat on the bench.

We held on through the first half, and as the third quarter ended, the Wolves were only up by five points. We had weathered their initial push, and more importantly, we were still in the game.

Could we finish a close playoff game for the second time against the best team in the league?

The nervousness and murmuring of the crowd was like an electrical current.

In the break between the third and fourth quarters, the team sat on the bench. For the first time during a game, I told them to close their eyes, sit up straight, and "breathe in through your nose, breathe out through your mouth."

For one full minute, in front of a packed crowd and a national television audience, before the fourth quarter of the biggest game of the year, we meditated.

The sounds of the crowd faded.

Let the wind blow me away . . .

20

TWO MINUTES

WE WERE DOWN three with 2:12 left and possession of the ball.

Sepo picked up Allan full court and called out the defensive switches for his teammates.

Good communication.

Allan passed into one of their post players, but the big man threw it to Mevin, who was sagging off to clog the paint.

Mevin took off and went full court with the ball. Fouled in the act of shooting.

There was 1:58 on the clock. We were down three, shooting two free throws.

Mevin made the first.

Down two.

Mevin missed the second, but Sepo jumped in between two Wolves players and pulled down the offensive rebound.

Sepo dribbled out and passed to Jack. Jack moved the ball to Mike, who attacked the basket. Jack looped wide to the top of the key, creating more space for Mike's drive. Mike passed back to Jack, who then swung it to Penda, wide open on the wing.

Sepo to Jack to Mike to Jack to Penda, everyone connected.

Penda, our sharpshooter, hit the open three.

We had scored four points in seconds. Just like that, the Wolves had gone from up three to down one.

There was 1:44 on the clock. Wolves took a timeout. The crowd was delirious.

Could this actually happen?

It would be the greatest upset in KBA history.

I sat on the bench. One older fan, excited and drunk, started shouting my name, trying to get my attention. The team huddled and talked to each other, while I sat present, in the moment, nonreactive.

"Ben! Ben!" came the shouts from the fan. I didn't move, didn't acknowledge that I heard anything.

The crowd didn't exist.

"Ben! Ben!"

The team was talking to each other, but I was too far away, and it was too loud, to hear what they were saying.

"Ben!"

The timeout ended and the huddle broke.

One hundred and four seconds left.

Allan came down and attacked the rim. Jack processed what was happening and left his man to take up space in the lane, camouflaged by a Wolves player in front of him. I had never seen someone do that before. Not only had Jack made the correct defensive read but he also hid himself behind Paulo so that Allan wouldn't know that Jack was there. As

Allan came in, Jack rose up and cleanly blocked his layup. The crowd cheered. For Allan, it must have seemed like Jack materialized out of nowhere.

We recovered the ball. Up one with 1:35 on the clock.

We inbounded the ball to Mike, who was supposed to be in Luderitz with his mom.

Sometimes Mike shot too much, but he had moxie about him and a feeling for the moment. He dribbled down the court, came off a little pick from Mevin, and pulled up for a three.

If Mike's shot went in, we would go up by four and be in a good position to win the game. If he missed, it would remain a one-point game, and the Wolves could easily score.

Mike's three-point shot arced high, and the crowd, mouths open, tracked the ball with their eyes.

As the players on the court were jockeying for rebounding position, the noise seemed to go out of the gym.

Mike's three swished through the net and, on the other side of the court, Sepo dropped two fingers down, making his little "count it" motion.

We were now up four with eighty-eight seconds left.

The fans were delirious, wanting to see this upset happen.

The Wolves scored. We were up two. Sepo brought the ball up and was fouled.

He stood at the line, forty seconds left in the game. If he made both of his free throws, we would go up four.

Sepo missed both shots.

The crowd groaned.

Still a two-point game.

The Wolves came down, missed, recovered the ball, and passed to Sky, the owner of the team. As Sky looked to the basket, about to take the potential game-winning three, Mike closed out hard, forcing Sky to pass. Allan caught the ball, twenty seconds left, and again attacked the basket. Jack, processing everything, rotated to Allan and blocked his shot. Again.

Sepo came up with the loose ball and passed ahead to Penda, who was fouled at half-court.

Our ball. Sideline-out-of-bounds. Sixteen seconds left. We were up two.

Sideline-out-of-bounds.

One word came to my mind. I said it twice.

"Boston. Boston."

Sepo came to the sideline to inbound the ball. Mevin moved to the backcourt. Jack, Penda, and Munya bunched up at the top of the key.

I felt it. We were going to beat the Wolves, and we were going to beat them with Boston.

Then the official sitting at the scorer's table called the two referees over. After a moment, they signaled two free throws. The Wolves were in the penalty, and rather than inbounding the ball, Penda would now shoot two free throws.

So much for Boston. If we were ever going to use it, that would have been the moment.

Penda stepped to the free throw line. If he hit both we would be up four with sixteen seconds left and in a good position to win the game.

Penda missed the first.

Now the Wolves would get the ball back with a chance to win or tie.

Penda hit the second.

We were up three.

Sixteen seconds left.

The Wolves inbounded to Allan. Sepo tracked him full court as Mike shaded behind Sepo, ready to double-team.

Jack waited under the basket, taking in everything, his computer processor of a brain calculating possibilities.

Allan dribbled hard down the court on the right side and stopped at the wing, behind the three-point line. Both Mike and Sepo were on him. Allan shot-faked, and Mike jumped, but Sepo, ever so clever, didn't bite. Allan rose up to shoot the game-tying three. Sepo, having waited for Allan's actual shot attempt, rose with him, hand straight up.

Allan, sensing he didn't have space to shoot, passed in mid-air to Paulo. Although Paulo was primarily a post-up player, he could shoot the three and was waiting for the ball at the top of the key.

As the pass was in mid-air, Jack had already started closing out on Paulo. Paulo caught the ball, and as he began to shoot, Jack was there, rising to contest Paulo's shot but smartly angling his body to Paulo's right side so that there would be no contact, no possibility of a foul being called.

Paulo, distracted by Jack, missed the shot. Mike got the rebound.

Five seconds left.

Allan grabbed Mike, fouling him.

We were up three with five seconds left. If Mike hit one of his free throws, we would go up four and win the game.

As a team, we had missed three of our four previous free throws.

Deep breath in . . .

Mike stood at the line, bent over, hands on his knees, waiting for the ref to pass him the ball.

Don't get too high or too low.

The ref, standing under the basket, checked the players lining up on either side of the lane, nodded to himself, and bounced the ball to Mike.

Mike caught the ball, took a deep breath, and shot the free throw.

The ball was high and looked like it was going to bounce off the back rim. Mike leaned back, willing it to go in.

The ball hit the back of the rim and dropped in.

Deep breath out . . .

Second shot.

Swish.

The Wolves came down and hit a shot, but it was too late. Time ran out. We had won the game by three points.

Sky collapsed to the ground in tears. The Blue Devils ran outside, fleeing the crowd flowing onto the court.

We had pulled off the greatest upset in KBA history.

As I made my way to the exit, Mpume, the coach of the Pacers, stopped me and said, "Wow."

His team, the Pacers, had won their series. We would meet in the Finals.

"Coach," said Mpume, "I think Sepo can play in South Africa." South Africa had the top professional league on the continent.

I thanked Mpume and made my way outside. The team was huddled together in laughter and disbelief.

I joined the huddle and said, "Mike, would you rather be in Luderitz?"

"No, Coach."

A few days later, Allan and I were back on the radio. The host asked Allan what happened.

"They got lucky," said Allan.

"Yes," I said. "It was a really lucky sweep."

21

BUZZER-BEATER

THE FINALS WERE ALSO a best-of-three series. In the regular season, we had split our series with the Pacers, each winning one game. Affiliated with the University of Namibia, Coach Mpume was a great teacher of the game but also didn't mind slapping a player on the back of the head if they weren't listening.

Concen-fucking-trate.

Although as coaches we were opposites, Mpume yelling out instructions from the sideline, we were also friends. Mpume was tall, maybe six foot six, and had dominated the game in his younger years, as well as having been a formidable rugby player.

Standing on the sideline, he resembled his nick-name, "The Great Elephant."

The Pacers were ten deep, and every player contributed. Their best player, Mike "Starter Pack" Mukuya, was a steward for Air Namibia. He was tall and athletic, able to rebound, dribble, and score from the post.

It was a Sunday afternoon game. The U.S. Ambassador to Namibia, whom I had come to know, sat in the front row.

Fourth quarter. We were down two with forty-one seconds left.

We pressed full court. The Pacers threw the ball ahead, and Sepo, with his long arms and huge hands, made a play and got the steal at half-court while falling to the floor. From the floor, Sepo passed to Mike, and Mike passed to Mevin on the wing.

Sepo was our leader, but Mevin was our best player. He was likely the quickest player in the KBA. As a team, we worked on boxing out. But Mevin didn't rebound by fundamentals; he outquicked everyone, jumping to the ball before other players left their feet. Although he was a star, Mevin hated the spotlight and avoided any attention people tried to give him. He was similar to Vincent in that all he wanted to do was be part of the team.

Mevin was quiet around me. When we talked, it was almost always about basketball.

Now with the ball, Mevin faked a shot and attacked the basket. He was fouled and hit both free throws.

Tie game with thirty-one seconds left.

We pressed again. The Pacers got the ball to Nigel, their primary ball handler. Sepo hounded Nigel and forced him into a turnover. I thought of those moments when I arrived early to practice and found Sepo already on the court, doing defensive slides with a brick in each hand.

Our ball. Fifteen seconds left. I was on the bench, not giving instructions or even saying anything.

Let the players play.

Mike brought the ball up and dribbled to the wing.

Seven seconds left.

Mike passed to Mevin on the baseline.

Five seconds.

Mevin turned, shot, and missed.

Three seconds.

Sepo out-jumped two Pacers and got the offensive rebound.

Two seconds.

Sepo took three dribbles out.

One second.

Sepo turned and fired a shot, two Pacers jumping to contest.

The buzzer sounded as the ball was in the air.

Swish.

The two referees signaled basket good.

Ballgame.

The team swarmed Sepo, showering him with hugs and high fives. Vincent led the charge, ripping his own jersey off in excitement.

A year ago, in the KBA, Sepo was a little-used backup forward. Now he was on national television, dominating the Finals.

We huddled up afterward, the team and I, our arms around each other, together.

꿁

After game one, the KBA community received tragic news. A player for the Poly Blues, the team we had beat for the final playoff spot, had died in a car accident.

The next day at practice, I told the team, "You never know when it is your time, so make sure you tell the people who are important in your life that you appreciate them."

Mevin had always been quiet and reserved around me, rarely sharing anything personal. That night he sent me a text that read, "Thanks for all you have done to help me. Appreciate that even though I never really show it. Thank you."

22

BOSTON

Before games, I met the team at the entrance to Augustineum High School, which was a central location relative to where most of the players lived. From there, four guys would pile into my car, and I'd pay for the rest to take a taxi to the University of Namibia.

As I was driving to Augustineum to pick up the guys before game two, I kept noticing the color blue. Several pedestrians were wearing blue scarves, one with a blue head wrap, another with a blue sweater. Everywhere I looked, blue was in the air.

A good sign.

When I arrived at the gates to Augustineum, the team was there, sitting on a short wall that ringed the school. Sepo was smiling. The team was loose and focused.

On the car ride to the University of Namibia, Shishani sang to us from the car speakers.

"For the first time I can feel it/I'm living in the moment..."

The first quarter went back and forth, and with three minutes left in the first, I pulled Mevin so he could get some rest. Mevin's game revolved around his quickness, which depended on maximum effort.

With Mevin on the bench, I worried about our scoring and rebounding. Sepo and Mevin had learned to run the pick and roll to perfection, and on defense, Mevin was our anchor, inhaling defensive rebounds.

For those three minutes at the end of the first quarter, with Mevin on the bench, Sepo recognized the moment and took over, setting his teammates up for open shots and encouraging them after each attempt, make or miss.

Confidence radiated from Sepo, and he moved like water, flowing into every space on the court. He had become a true playmaker, attuned to what the team needed at any given time and always attempting to fill that need.

It was beautiful to watch.

We kept the momentum and started the fourth quarter leading by six points. Throughout the fourth, the Pacers played with the frantic energy of a team on the brink of elimination.

With 1:07 left, we were up by five points and shooting two free throws.

I took my final timeout. We stood and meditated in the huddle. With our arms around each other, I literally felt the heartbeat of the player next to me slow down.

The team went back onto the court. Munya hit one of two.

We were up six.

The Pacers came down and scored.

Up four. One minute left.

Sepo missed a three. Munya got the rebound and was fouled. He made one of two.

Up five. Forty-five seconds on the clock.

The Pacers came down and quickly scored.

Three-point game. Thirty-eight seconds left.

Mevin missed a three. Munya tipped the ball to Sepo. Sepo missed a contested layup.

The ball was batted out of bounds. Our ball. Up three. Twenty seconds left.

Sideline-out-of-bounds.

It took me a second to process the time and situation.

Sideline-out-of-bounds.

"Boston. Boston."

The Pacers were a desperate team, at the end of a game, needing to get a steal. This was the precise situation for which Boston had been designed.

Sepo stood in front of me on the sideline, waiting for the referee to hand him the ball. We had run through Boston so many times, the team moved into position as if it were just another end of practice.

Mevin backed up and waited in the backcourt. He knew he was getting the ball but betrayed no hint to his defender, Starter Pack, who guarded him closely.

Jack, Penda, and Munya bunched up together at the top of the three-point line.

The official handed the ball to Sepo. He had five seconds to inbound.

Sepo slapped the ball.

And then, nothing. The three players bunched up at the three-point line stood there, waiting.

In the heat of competition, at the end of a close contest, players and teams can sometimes self-sabotage, scared to give all their effort and still lose.

In their stillness, I sensed this self-sabotage was happening.

"Go!" I shouted. For the players, my shout must have been unexpected. During games, I had hardly raised my voice, and often, I said nothing. Now I shouted to break them out of their daze.

"Go!" I yelled again

The players *went*.

Penda and Jack cut to the wings.

Two seconds passed.

I sat down, completely calm, certain the play would work.

Munya turned and set a pick for Mevin.

Three seconds passed, the ref extending his arm to indicate each passing second.

Mevin V-cut backward, his defender sticking to him as planned, and began his run to the basket.

Then something unexpected happened, something for which we had never planned: the man guarding Jack didn't follow Jack out to the wing. Instead, he was waiting in the lane, watching the play develop, ready to break up any action toward the basket.

Mpume, the coach of the Pacers, had recognized the general outlines of what we were going to do and knew there would be some sort of action toward the basket. He was yelling and pointing, indicating that the defender guarding Jack should stay in the lane.

If a defender was in the lane, waiting for Mevin, the play would fall apart. It would potentially be a turnover, and the Pacers would have possession with plenty of time to score and send the game to overtime.

We had never practiced for this possibility.

I could stand up and instruct some other pass, direct the action from the sidelines as other coaches did, but that would likely distract the players and increase the chances of a turnover. In the split-second that this happened, as much unconsciously as consciously, I chose to do nothing.

I sat on the bench and watched the play unfold.

This was the culmination of my two years of coaching in Namibia.

Jack, who processed things so quickly, recognized that his defender hadn't followed him to the three-point line. Improvising, Jack casually waved for the ball. Jack's wave was the critical piece of the entire play. It was so subtle that I would only see it later while rewatching the game on my laptop.

Jack's defender, seeing Jack wave—not a grand, "Look, I'm open!" gesture but rather a subtle, small movement—assumed the pass was going to Jack. He closed out hard on Jack and left the lane open.

The referee extended his arm.

Four seconds.

Sepo pass-faked as we had done many times in practice, working through basketball movements slowly, without a ball, grooving that knowledge and building that myelin. The defender guarding the inbounds jumped, biting on Sepo's pass-fake, knowing that five seconds was almost up.

The referee's arm was now halfway extended for the fifth time. We were a less than a second away from a violation. Mindful of the time, Sepo lobbed a high-arcing pass toward the empty space in front of our basket.

There was a gasp from the crowd. It looked like Sepo had just passed the ball to no one, had turned it over in the final moments of a close game.

Mevin was running now and passed Munya shoulder-to-shoulder at the top of the three-point line. Munya picked off Mevin's defender.

With each individual defender closely guarding Jack and Penda on the wings, and with Mevin's defender picked off by Munya, the lane was suddenly, magically, wide open.

The ball hung in the air.

Mevin caught it in stride and made an easy layup.

Five-point game. The clock ran out and the buzzer sounded.

We had won.

The Blue Devils Basketball Club had swept our way to the championship. We may have been .500 during the regular season, but in the playoffs, we were undefeated.

In the deciding moments of the championship game, we sealed our win with Boston, a play we had never before run in a game, a play that depended on one of our players improvising on the spot.

I thought back to that parking lot across from the Wanaheda Police Station, sitting with Sepo, Shishani singing softly in the background, talking about starting our own team.

"Blue Devils for life," he had said.

Throughout the season, I encouraged the team over and over again to stay in the moment. We wouldn't get too high when we won, and we wouldn't get too low when we lost.

When the buzzer sounded, and the championship was official, I clapped once. Sepo pumped his fist. Vincent, the hero of game one against the Wolves, came out and hugged Sepo. Munya and Mevin bumped fists. Penda pulled his jersey over his head in disbelief. Jack simply walked off the court.

No one looked at the cheering crowd giving us a standing ovation.

Melissa, a friend of mine, later said to me, "You were so low-key I thought there was still one more quarter left."

When I watched Boston later, rewinding it again and again on my laptop, I noticed something else besides Jack's improvisational wave.

When Mevin scored, the first player to jump off the bench in excitement was Vincent.

23

SIX YEARS LATER

WE WERE on the same outdoor court with the same sounds of the nearby soccer game wafting through the air.

I was standing with Jack. On the first day of practice, six years ago, he was so new to the game that he tripped and fell doing a basic defensive shuffle.

Now Jack was a star in the KBA, a tall, athletic point guard who could dunk easily and finish with either hand. He was also a volunteer coach, teaching the game to high schoolers, some of whom had never before played.

I had retired from coaching four years earlier.

Except for today.

Jack texted me, asking if I could I help him with some of the drills we used to run.

As I stood on the court, the happy shouts of soccer in the distance, the sun shining down, and my mind flipping back and forth between the past and present, I felt so much happiness, so much content-ment from watching Jack walk his new players through the same drills we used to do.

First, we had the team line up in rows. No basket-balls. V-cut. Rebound. Form shooting. Everything in slow motion. Groove that knowledge.

The night before, Mike had sent me a message. He worked on the coast now and, similar to Jack, had started coaching a high school team. Mike's message read, "I taught them Boston today. That play is embedded . . . Those memories stick with me forever. Deep breath in, deep breath out. Best coaching advice ever. Still have all of your principles and that's how I'll be coaching."

As a teenager, Mike's first option had always been Mike. Now, as a young man, he was applying one of the lessons he had learned: a team is about being part of something bigger than yourself, and coaching is about more than basketball.

Jack and I had the high schoolers work on layups, finishing with either hand. No dribble. One, two, jump.

Mevin had dropped out of university and moved back home to work on the family farm, far to the north.

Following our instructions, each player slapped five with the rest of the team as they ran to the end of the layup line to begin again.

Vincent was an entrepreneur. Twenty-three years old, wearing a business suit, calling people on his cell phone with this deal or that. He no longer played basketball. Sometimes he would come over to my apartment and practice his latest pitch.

Penda, our handsome sharpshooter, was in medical school in Cuba. He DM'd me, out of the blue, saying that he still practiced meditation.

The sun was getting low. We let the team play three-on-three.

Munya was still playing in the KBA. He signed all of his text messages with one word: Boston.

Jack walked around the court, watching the players as I used to do.

Sepo did not go on to play in South Africa. He started drinking too much, and his uncle kicked him out of the house. Sepo moved back to his village, twelve hours north of Windhoek. Every now and then I would get a scrap of information—he was working on a farm; he was messed up with drugs. Sepo didn't have the internet or a cell phone or even, likely, electricity.

I had no way to reach him in a part of the country where homesteads are still thatched-roof huts with open-air kitchens. He was an orphan again, with no steady employment, living alone in a small village in rural Africa.

Life doesn't have Hollywood endings.

The wheatgrass swayed. It had been cut and grown and cut and grown, over and over again.

I took Jack aside at the end of practice and reminded him of the most important lesson in coaching.

"After high school, a lot of these guys will stop playing," I said. "They will forget what you taught them. But they will always remember how you made them feel."

"Yes, Coach," said Jack, as polite and receptive as ever.

Basketball is a season that ends, sooner or later, for every player. It's the relationships that matter, not the wins and losses. When I focused on that and not on winning, I won more than I ever had.

As practice finished, I thanked the players, said goodbye to Jack, and walked to my car.

There is a circular path to life. Those we teach carry our lessons forward. The circle repeats, with a touch more knowledge and wisdom.

I sat in the driver's seat and closed the door. The sounds of soccer and basketball faded.

The team is gone now, but the lessons we had learned together remain.

We are all connected.

Blue Devils.

My eyes teared up as I drove away.

Deep breath in. Deep breath out.

For life.

AFTERWORD

After completing the final draft and sending the book for copy edits I received a Facebook Message from Sepo.

He is back in Windhoek and seems to be doing better.

I explained the book and asked if Sepo would like me to use a pseudonym for his "character."

He replied, "Truth n facts coach."

I thanked him and Sepo replied with, "Welcome n thank u for everything. Every lesson on n off the court coach."

ACKNOWLEDGMENTS

I started this book in March of 2021 in my two-bedroom apartment in Windhoek, Namibia, looking out over my small garden. I finished the final draft in New York in my parents' apartment overlooking the Hudson River on October 5, 2021.

David Friedman was my first reader. Emailing back and forth with David, he in Dayton, Ohio, and me in Namibia, helped clarify my goals for the book.

Annah Kuriakose was my second reader and first editor. She encouraged me to both expand and focus the story. Her assistance was invaluable. As is her friendship.

Glenn Stout was my third reader and second editor. Growing up, my father and I loved *The Best American Sports Writing* and gifted it to each other every Christmas. Glenn Stout was the series editor. As I was revising the manuscript, quarantining in New York after leaving Namibia, on a whim, I Googled Glenn, found his contact info, setup a call, and, within a few days, was working with a professional editor of the highest order. Emailing and calling Glenn every few weeks was like having a master teacher giving a masterclass in nonfiction narrative. And I made a new friend. Double lucky.

Finally, thank you to my parents, who served both as early readers and, more importantly, pillars of unconditional love.

Ben Guest

Head Coach, Ret.

Blue Devils Basketball Club

NEWSLETTER

Join the hundreds of people who have signed up for my free weekly newsletter at benbo.substack.com for interviews with writers AND receive a FREE copy of my ebook *Lessons Learned Self-Publishing on Amazon, Working with a Professional Editor, Starting a Podcast, and Creating a Newsletter.*

REVIEW

I hope you enjoyed this book.

Please consider leaving a review of this book on Amazon.

Thank you.

-Ben Guest

ABOUT THE AUTHOR

Ben Guest was born in Vermont and lives in New York City.